**Quick and Easy Guide: Bible Prophecy**

# Quick and Easy Guide
# Bible Prophecy

## Brian R. Coffey

**Tyndale House Publishers, Inc.**
WHEATON, ILLINOIS

Edited by Susan Taylor
Designed by Melinda Schumacher

**Library of Congress Cataloging-in-Publication Data**

Coffey, Brian R., date
        The quick and easy guide to Bible prophecy / Brian R. Coffey.
            p.   cm.
        Includes bibliographical references.
        ISBN 0-8423-3842-X (sc)
        1. Bible–Prophecies–End of the world.   2. End of the world–
Biblical teaching.   3. Eschatology–Biblical teaching.   I. Title
BS649.E63C63   1999
220.1′5–dc21                                                              99-22608

Printed in the United States of America

05   04   03   02   01   00
7     6     5     4

*To the people that are First Baptist Church of Geneva:*

*May we continue to
believe, belong, and become
together.*

# Table of Contents

# Acknowledgments

*It's been said that it takes a village to raise a child. While I'm sure there's a good bit of truth to that, I'm also sure it takes a whole group of people to make a book! I want to thank my friend Ron Beers, executive vice president of Tyndale House Publishers and church softball league teammate, for encouraging me to develop the idea that became this book. I am thankful as well for the skillful editing of Susan Taylor, who brought shape and clarity to the project. Finally, I want to thank Dr. Timothy Weber for his willingness to read and lend his expertise to this manuscript.*

*On a more personal level, I am forever grateful for the love and example of my parents, Roland and Joan Coffey. After nearly fifty years of ministry together, they still begin each day with the words "Today could be the day Jesus returns!" I thank God for giving me two biological brothers, who also became spiritual brothers: Joe, a pastor, who shares the thrill and struggles of ministry, and our late little brother, John, who left us far too early but who is at home today in heaven. Finally, words cannot express the love and support I receive daily from my wife, Lorene, and our four boys, Jordan, Jesse, Micah, and Canaan. Thank you all for filling my days with such joy.*

# Introduction

Thirty-nine bodies, all neatly and identically dressed, were found lying dead in their beds in a sprawling suburban home in California. The nation was horrified in March 1997 by the gruesome discovery at the headquarters of the Heaven's Gate cult. Although any such event is tragic, this one seemed particularly sad because cult members, led by charismatic New Age guru Marshall Herff Applewhite, had poisoned themselves in an apparent mass suicide. While the cult's bizarre doctrines defy simple explanation, its members seem to have believed that the appearance of the spectacular Hale-Bopp comet signaled the end of the world. Applewhite and his followers took their own lives in order to rendezvous with a spaceship they believed traveled with the comet and would take them to what they called "the Evolutionary Level Above Human." In an article in *Time* magazine, Elizabeth Gleick wrote: "Students of the millennium and historians of the bizarre have long been predicting such a catastrophic event in the twilight years of the 20th century, duly noting the rise of obscure cults and the increasingly fevered pitch of their rantings."[1]

If Ms. Gleick is right, and I believe she is, we will find ourselves inundated with what might be called "millennial hysteria" in the months leading up to the year 2000. The dawn of the third millennium will cause millions to wonder, *Is the world near the end? And if the end is near, how and when will it come?* Such renewed interest in eschatology (the study of the end times) will cause scoffing and ridicule at one end of the spectrum and the rise of groups like Heaven's Gate at the other. Along with this renewed spiritual interest will come great confusion about the purpose and truth of Bible prophecy. While the increased interest is good, the confusion is frightening. Scores of books will be published, and hundreds of articles will be written. Some of these will be anchored in biblical truth; others will be sensational speculation. How will we be able to discern what is true and what is false, to distinguish dangerous cults from sound Christian groups? How can we prevent our children and friends from being swept up in seemingly informed, even very committed, groups that are, nonetheless, terribly wrong? Bible prophecy is of extraordinary significance because if it is true, it provides authoritative answers to these questions and many more!

If you were going to travel to Paris, France, or St. Petersburg, Russia, and you had only two days to stay there, a good guide would tell you the must-sees of your brief visit. You would then be able to use your available time to get an overview and a flavor of the magnificence of the city. That's what this book seeks to do with the topic of prophecy. It's easy to become confused—or to be put off completely—by the diagrams, charts, and complex theories that attempt to predict how and when certain events will occur, and we could spend a lifetime studying those things. So how can we condense what is an enormously complex and confusing topic into the basic truths essential to an understanding of what the Bible teaches about the subject? That is the purpose of this book: to outline what anyone—from the committed Christian to the spiritually curious to the agnostic—needs to know about Bible prophecy.

I have tried to approach this book with twin priorities: to be faithful to the Word of God and to make the basic truths of Bible prophecy understandable to any reader. It is my hope and prayer that you will grasp these fundamental truths in a way that will strengthen your faith—or help you come to faith, enable you to recognize unbiblical teaching, and cause you to anticipate with greater joy the coming of our glorious Lord and King, Jesus Christ.

# 1 Prophecy and the Past:
## The End of the World As We Know It

*Then the seventh angel poured out his bowl into the air. And a mighty shout came from the throne of the Temple in heaven, saying, "It is finished!" Then the thunder crashed and rolled, and lightning flashed. And there was an earthquake greater than ever before in human history. The great city of Babylon split into three pieces, and cities around the world fell into heaps of rubble.*

REVELATION 16:17-19

At the beginning of each new year the supermarket tabloids explode with sensational headlines:

## *Millennium 2000: The Beginning of the End?!*
## *New Proof That We're in the Biblical Last Days!*

Every year thousands upon thousands of people in North America call in or log on to organizations such as the Psychic Friends Network, seeking answers to questions concerning their personal future:

1

Will I fall in love? Will I find a new job? Will I enjoy good health?

We may laugh and shake our head at the wild claims of the tabloids, and perhaps we would not think of consulting a psychic, but we may wish we could see into the future. What great world events are going to happen in the next year? Will a comet crash into our planet? Will there be a major war? Will the stock market crash? Will my favorite baseball team win the World Series? If we are honest, most of us wonder about the future, but we usually keep our questions to ourselves.

The truth is, no human being can see into the future. Our vision is limited to the past and the present. The future is the realm of God, and to the extent that we are able to understand it, prophecy is the mechanism God has chosen to reveal the future to us.

## The Place of Prophecy in the Bible

The Bible is chock-full of prophecies, including hundreds, if not thousands, of predictive prophecies. From cover to cover, from Genesis to Revelation, prophecy plays a major role in God's relationship with the world he created. Following the story of the Creation in Genesis 1–2, the serpent tempts Adam and Eve to disobey God's restriction against eating from the tree of the knowledge of good and evil. After Adam and Eve sin, God outlines the consequences of disobedience and pronounces a curse on the serpent as the representative of Satan. In God's rebuke of the serpent, we see a foretelling of Christ's ultimate victory over Satan: "So the Lord God said to the serpent, '. . . From now on, you and the woman will be enemies, and your offspring and her offspring will be enemies. He will crush your head, and you will strike his heel'" (Genesis 3:14-15).

But Bible prophecy is not limited to apocalyptic visions of the destruction of Satan and the end of the world. In fact, prophecy often focuses on rather routine historical events, from the lives of individual people to the interactions of nations. Among the most frequent and significant topics of Bible prophecy is the nation of Israel. Long before Israel even existed, God promised to bless Abram with descendants who would become a great nation, and through that nation (Israel) God would bless the whole world:

> The Lord told Abram, "Leave your country, your relatives, and your father's house, and go to the land that I will show you. I will cause you to become the father of a great nation. I will bless you and make you famous, and I will make you a blessing to others. I will bless those who bless you and curse those who curse you. All the families of the earth will be blessed through you." (Genesis 12:1-3)

The New Testament teaches that God's prophecy to Abram was ultimately fulfilled by the birth, death, and resurrection of Jesus, the one called the king of the Jews. Scores of prophecies predicted that the Messiah of God, the Anointed One, the Son of God, would come into the world as

Savior, High Priest, and King—and that he would be born in Israel.

> For a child is born to us, a son is given to us. And the government will rest on his shoulders. These will be his royal titles: Wonderful Counselor, Mighty God, Everlasting Father, Prince of Peace. His ever expanding, peaceful government will never end. He will rule forever with fairness and justice from the throne of his ancestor David. The passionate commitment of the Lord Almighty will guarantee this! (Isaiah 9:6-7)

Predictive prophecy of the Bible points not only to the coming of Christ as Savior but also to the establishment of his church. Before his death and resurrection, Jesus, speaking to Peter, prophesied, "Now I say to you that you are Peter, and upon this rock I will build my church, and all the powers of hell will not conquer it" (Matthew 16:18). Despite many predictions of its demise, the church of Jesus Christ has endured for nearly two thousand years and is stronger today than at any other point in history. When we read prophecies that have already been fulfilled, we gain confidence that prophecies not yet fulfilled will also come to pass.

The culmination of all Bible prophecy is to be found in Revelation, the last book of the Bible. In a magnificent series of visions, the apostle John gives us a glimpse into what is yet to come. The following passages include prophecies about the triumphant second coming of Jesus Christ, the end of world history, and the glorious promise of heaven:

> Look! He comes with the clouds of heaven. And everyone will see him— even those who pierced him. And all the nations of the earth will weep because of him. Yes! Amen!
>
> "I am the Alpha and the Omega— the beginning and the end," says the Lord God. "I am the one who is, who always was, and who is still to come, the Almighty One." (Revelation 1:7-8)

No temple could be seen in the city,
for the Lord God Almighty and the
Lamb are its temple. And the city has
no need of sun or moon, for the glory
of God illuminates the city, and the
Lamb is its light. (Revelation 21:22-23)

But before we jump headlong into the dramatic images of the prophetic future, let's
take a look at the function of prophecy in
the past.

## Handwriting on the Wall of History

Prophecy goes beyond the forecasting of
cataclysmic spiritual events to predict many
events in "secular" political history. Most of
us are familiar with the phrase "the handwriting on the wall." If, for example, we see
a friend consistently showing up to work
late or failing to achieve even minimal
performance standards, we might say, "The
handwriting is on the wall—he or she is
going to be fired." Many people are not
aware that this phrase has its origin in the
Old Testament.

Throughout the Bible the great city of

Babylon, located in modern-day Iraq, is representative of all that is pagan and godless in the world. It was filled with idols and all manner of evil. In the fifth chapter of Daniel we read that King Belshazzar was in the middle of a great party when he and all his guests saw the fingers of a human hand writing on the plaster wall of the king's palace. "The king himself saw the hand as it wrote, and his face turned pale with fear. Such terror gripped him that his knees knocked together and his legs gave way beneath him" (Daniel 5:5-6).

King Belshazzar had heard that Daniel had a reputation for great wisdom and discernment. So the king called on Daniel to reveal to him the meaning of the mysterious writing. Daniel was a prophet, and God used him to speak to Belshazzar:

> Your Majesty, the Most High God gave sovereignty, majesty, glory, and honor to your predecessor, Nebuchadnezzar. He made him so great that people of all races and nations and languages trembled before him in fear. . . . But

when his heart and mind were hardened with pride, he was brought down from his royal throne and stripped of his glory. . . . You are his successor, O Belshazzar, and you knew all this, yet you have not humbled yourself. For you have defied the Lord of heaven. . . . You have not honored the God who gives you the breath of life and controls your destiny! So God has sent this hand to write a message.

This is the message that was written: Mene, Mene, Tekel, Parsin. This is what these words mean:

*Mene* means "numbered"—God has numbered the days of your reign and has brought it to an end.

*Tekel* means "weighed"—you have been weighed on the balances and have failed the test.

*Parsin* means "divided"—your kingdom has been divided and given to the Medes and Persians. (Daniel 5:18-28)

That very night, the Bible says, Belshazzar was killed, and Darius the Mede took over his kingdom. Prophecy was literally the handwriting on the wall for King Belshazzar. But this account is included in the Bible not just to make fascinating reading. God's prophets and their prophecies still declare the blessings of obeying God and forewarn us of the consequences of disregarding his truth.

How can we begin to grasp such an astonishing body of ancient literature? The most popular way to deal with Bible prophecy, especially as we approach the dawn of the third millennium, is to attempt to use prophecy to predict future world events. People have written scores of books with this focus. The problem is, there are so many prophecies, and world history is so complex, that trying to make sense of it all can quickly become overwhelming. In the 1960s many who wrote books on the subject felt sure that the former Soviet Union was the country most likely to be the great enemy of God. In the 1980s the Soviet

Union disintegrated, and now the focus has shifted to Iran and Iraq.

When it comes to prophecy, sometimes it is easy to miss the forest because of the trees; that is, to focus on the details instead of on the larger picture. But if we begin with the view that the primary purpose of prophecy is to communicate the truth of God, and in particular the truth about Jesus Christ, everything else becomes secondary.

## The Purpose of Prophecy

Like many other people, I hate to go to the dentist. I once went thirteen years (from age nineteen to age thirty-two) without making a single dental appointment! But after seeing an infomercial on gum disease, I reluctantly made an appointment. As it turned out, I had only one cavity, but the dentist asked me a strange question: "Do you grind your teeth at night?" I told her that I wasn't aware of doing it but my wife had occasionally mentioned that I did. The dentist went on to tell me that she could see hundreds of tiny hairline cracks on the surface of my teeth—evidence that I did grind my teeth. Then she said, "If you continue to do this without doing something about it, your teeth will eventually begin to crack, and you'll be looking at dentures." What she gave me (in addition to a plastic night guard to wear when I sleep) was a prophecy concerning my teeth.

In his book *The Final Drama,* Bible scholar John F. Walvoord writes:

> Prophecy is that part of Scripture dealing with predictions of events that will occur in the future. Theologians call this doctrine *eschatology,* a word derived from the Greek *eschatos,* meaning "last" or "last things." It refers to the events that will climax human history. Included in biblical eschatology are all predictions that were future at the time they were written, whether they have been fulfilled now or are still unfulfilled.[1]

In order to understand and interpret prophecy, we need to keep several principles in mind.

## *Prophecy Reminds Us That God Is Sovereign*

In the book of Daniel, the Babylonian king Nebuchadnezzar became proud and exulted in his greatness. So God humbled him by causing him to become insane for a time. After God restored Nebuchadnezzar to his right mind, the king responded with a clear testimony to God's sovereignty:

> After this time had passed, I, Nebuchadnezzar, looked up to heaven. My sanity returned, and I praised and worshiped the Most High and honored the one who lives forever.
>
> His rule is everlasting, and his kingdom is eternal.
> All the people of the earth are nothing compared to him.
> He has the power to do as he pleases among the angels of heaven and with those who live on earth.
> No one can stop him or challenge him, saying, "What do you mean by doing these things?" (Daniel 4:34-35)

God is all-powerful (omnipotent), all-knowing (omniscient), and eternal (unbound by time), and therefore, even though he has allowed humanity the gift of free will, God rules supreme.

Over and over again God's faithful prophets thunder out the warning that human beings are not in control of the universe. In spite of the freedom God has allowed us, he reserves the right to exercise his authority and power to accomplish his will whenever and however he chooses. Prophecy is a powerful reminder of who God is.

## *Prophecy Reminds Us That the Word of God Is True, Accurate, and Reliable*

My wife and I typically tune in to the ten o'clock news in the evening. We usually watch until we've seen the weather forecast before we go to bed. Even though the meteorologist's predictions are not 100 percent correct (we live near Chicago so a 50 percent accuracy rate would probably be generous!), we still pay attention and plan the next day's activities accordingly.

If tomorrow's weather is different from today's forecast, it's not that important. But if the events predicted in the Bible rarely came to pass, Bible prophecy would be meaningless. If those prophecies were never fulfilled, we could have no real confidence in Scripture as the inspired and completely trustworthy Word of God. The Bible would be no more reliable than one of those supermarket tabloids. The fact is, when the Bible predicts events, they do happen! Scholars estimate that about half of all the predictive prophecies in the Bible have already been fulfilled![2] Therefore, we can have great confidence not only that the remaining prophecies will come to pass but also that the Bible can be trusted in other areas as well.

Human beings may choose to live by God's revealed Word or to disregard it, but it remains—and holds—the key to the destiny of every human soul. Through the prophet Jeremiah, God warned, "Listen, all the earth! I will bring disaster upon my people. It is the fruit of their own sin because they refuse to listen to me. They have rejected all my instructions" (Jeremiah 6:19). The fulfillment of this prophecy occurred when the Babylonians invaded and overwhelmed Judah (the southern kingdom of Israel, including the great city Jerusalem) in 586 B.C.—an event described in Jeremiah 39. When God's prophets speak in the Bible, those words are every bit as binding and eternal as the law of gravity or the laws of thermodynamics. Prophecy is a powerful reminder that God's Word is true and reliable.

## *Prophecy Calls Us to Spiritual and Moral Obedience to God's Word*

As the parents of four energy-packed, rambunctious young sons, my wife and I have had to establish certain ground rules about the boys' activities. For example, in the house we do not permit the boys to play games that involve kicking (the patched holes in our basement walls testify to the necessity for this rule). As long as the boys adhere to this rule, they have fun, and Mom and Dad are happy. If they violate the law, three things happen: (1) Someone usually gets hurt (a corollary rule is, No bleeding in the house); (2) Mom and Dad are profoundly unhappy; and (3) punishment is swift and just. In a sense, then, when my wife and I say to our sons, "You can play in the basement, but remember, *no kicking!*" we are standing in the great tradition of prophecy.

After the exodus from Egypt, the people of Israel spent forty years wandering through the wilderness because they failed to obey God's commands. When at last they stood on the brink of entering the land God had promised to give them, God spoke through Moses to remind the people of the purpose of his words to them. In Deuteronomy 6:3 we read, "Listen closely, Israel, to everything I say. Be careful to obey. Then all will go well with you, and you will have many children in the land flowing with milk and honey, just as the Lord, the God of your ancestors, promised you."

We could say that Bible prophecy is both a *diagnosis* and a *prognosis*. Picture this all-too-common scenario: A fifty-five-year-old man goes to his doctor for a physical checkup. He is forty pounds overweight, has blood pressure of 190/30, high cholesterol, and has smoked three packs of cigarettes a day for the past twenty years. After examining the patient, the doctor offers a diagnosis of the man's problem: an unhealthy lifestyle characterized by smoking, a lack of exercise, and poor eating habits. Then the doctor offers his prognosis: "If you don't make some changes, you are in serious trouble!" Through his faithful prophets, God did essentially the same thing. He diagnosed the problem (sin) and gave the prognosis (if people continued to disobey him, the result would be judgment). Prophecy is like a road sign that says: Caution! Sharp Curve Ahead. Reduce Speed! We would be foolish to ignore such a sign.

So what are the signs God has posted? The book of Daniel is best known for the account of Daniel in the lions' den, one of the first Bible stories children learn in Sunday school. But Daniel is also a prophetic book that illustrates each of the purposes of Bible prophecy. Most scholars believe Daniel was written in the middle of the sixth century B.C. as a historical account of the Babylonian captivity of the Jews. But as Daniel, a gifted prophet of God, continued to faithfully deliver the words of God to the most powerful men on earth (the Babylonian rulers), God also revealed his redemptive plan for history. Thus, the book of Daniel, like much of prophecy, can be read on several levels. It contains a historical account of real people and real historical situations. It includes prophecy concerning the ancient kingdom of Babylon and the nation of Israel. And, seen from the perspective of faith, it paints a prophetic picture of the distant future, a future that draws ever nearer in our own time.

Through a number of spectacular dreams and visions, Daniel predicted the rise and fall of a series of great world empires. As people looking back over history from our perspective on the brink of the twenty-first century, we can point to the ancient kingdoms of Babylon, Medo-

Persia, Greece, and Rome as fulfilling Daniel's prophecies.

Throughout the prophecies of Daniel, God emphasizes that he alone is sovereign. Though the great kingdoms of the world have tremendous power—much of it influenced by the evil one—they will one day crumble under the hand of the God who rules with absolute authority.

## The End of the World Is a Sure Thing

Most of us have heard the old saying by Benjamin Franklin, "In this world nothing can be said to be certain, except death and taxes." Bible prophecy would agree with at least half of that statement. We may or may not have to pay taxes, but we can count on death as a sure thing. All life comes to an end sooner or later.

Many Eastern philosophies hold what might be called a cyclical view of history. That is, history is seen as an endless, recurring cycle in which nothing ever changes. In his book *The Future Explored,* Dr. Timothy P. Weber, academic dean of Northern Baptist Theological Seminary, writes:

In many traditional Eastern cultures, this cyclical view has combined with certain religious ideas to make human progress almost impossible. In India, for example, the Hindu concept of *karma* holds that a person's present condition in life is the result of the good or bad which he committed in a previous existence.[3]

Human history, seen from the same perspective, has no end but is rather an endless repetitive cycle of events.

In contrast, the Bible teaches that history is *linear* and *redemptive*. History is linear in that, according to Christian theology, it is not an endless cycle of repeated events but, rather, has a beginning ("In the beginning, God created . . ."); a middle (the incarnation, death, and resurrection of Christ and life as we know it); and an end (the second coming of Christ and the end of time as we know it). History is also redemptive in that God is sovereign and will one day restore all of creation to the fullness of its intended purpose. If we use the language of Daniel, the handwriting on the wall reveals that history has a purpose and is moving toward a final destination.

Hardly a year goes by that we don't hear news of massive forest fires raging out of control or the devastating impact of earthquakes, floods, or famines on nearly every continent on the globe. Some observers point to such things as indicators that the earth is nearing an end. Others speculate that cataclysmic changes in world politics and economics could give rise to a renegade military or political leader who could effectively hold the world hostage by threatening nuclear holocaust or financial meltdown. We find ourselves wondering, Could all this be a sign of global catastrophe? Could this be the beginning of the end?

Some of us are old enough to remember the bomb drills we went through at school at the height of the Cuban missile crisis in 1962. I remember thinking it was fun to crawl under my desk and cover my head with my hands. Little did I know that my parents sometimes wondered whether there would be another day. Through prophecy,

Jesus taught that human history as we know it is not cyclical but linear—it will have an end. In Matthew 24:3 the disciples asked the Lord, "When will all this take place? And will there be any sign ahead of time to signal your return and the end of the world?" To their questions, Jesus responded,

> "Don't let anyone mislead you. For many will come in my name, saying, 'I am the Messiah.' They will lead many astray. And wars will break out near and far, but don't panic. Yes, these things must come, but the end won't follow immediately. The nations and kingdoms will proclaim war against each other, and there will be famines and earthquakes in many parts of the world. But all this will be only the beginning of the horrors to come." (Matthew 24:4-8)

> "Now, learn a lesson from the fig tree. When its buds become tender and its leaves begin to sprout, you know with-

out being told that summer is near.
Just so, when you see the events I've
described beginning to happen, you
can be sure that his return is very near,
right at the door." (Mark 13:28-29)

Just as my dentist pointed out the hairline cracks that spelled trouble for my
teeth, so prophecy reveals the stress frac-
tures in human history. Although modern-day prognosticators come to erroneous
conclusions concerning the end of history,
it is difficult to escape the sense that the
world as we know it is building a kind of
cataclysmic momentum—somewhat like a
tidal wave of global forces that are seemingly intent on fulfilling Jesus' words in the
not-too-distant future. A person could
spend weeks digging out all of the Bible's
prophetic utterances concerning the end
of the world, but simply put, the Bible
teaches that human history is rushing
toward completion and that by the very
nature of time itself, we are closer to the
end today than we have ever been before.
Speaking at a men's retreat at our

church, Stephen Arterburn, cofounder
and chairman of New Life Clinics, told
the story of a guy who went scuba diving
in the beautiful Pacific Ocean off the
coast of California. He expected to spend
the day enjoying the cool water and the
exhilaration of experiencing nature in
its pristine form. It was at a time when
scorching summer temperatures and dry
weather had caused a number of fires.
Authorities responsible for fighting the
fires called into service planes capable of
scooping up thousands of gallons of water
out of the sea and dropping it on the
fires. You can probably see where this
story is going! A tanker plane scooped up
this poor scuba diver with the seawater
and dropped him to his death on a raging
forest fire! Although I have not been able
to confirm the accuracy of this bizarre
story, I can say with certainly that we all
have something in common with that
scuba diver: We don't know when the
end is coming!

As significant as the question of the end
of world history is, there is an even more

important—and more personal—question each of us must be prepared to answer. As we think about our own life, it becomes uncomfortably clear that, while the world as you and I know it might continue, there is a clear possibility that our participation in it—that is, your life and mine—will end within the next fifty to seventy years. How can I be so sure? It is both medically and mathematically probable that we will all face death within that time frame. As my brother Joe says, "The human mortality rate is still hovering right around 100 percent." So whether or not the world ends as a result of nuclear destruction, environmental decay, or the impact of a giant meteor, each of us will die. And when we do, we will face eternity. The writer of the book of Hebrews reminds us:

> Just as it is destined that each person dies only once and after that comes judgment, so also Christ died only once as a sacrifice to take away the sins of many people. He will come again but not to deal with our sins again.

This time he will bring salvation to all those who are eagerly waiting for him. (Hebrews 9:27-28)

Bible prophecy tells us in a hundred ways that just as human history will end, so also our life is finite and will come to an end. One day, perhaps in the not-too-distant future, you and I will meet God face-to-face. Prophecy tells us that if we disregard this fact and ignore the truth of God, we will not only experience the pain of sin in this life but will also be unprepared to enter the next life.

# 2 Prophecy and the Future:
## The King of Kings and the Great Enemy

*That day will not come until there is a great
rebellion against God and the man of lawlessness is revealed—the one who brings destruction.
He will exalt himself and defy every god there is
and tear down every object of adoration and
worship. He will position himself in the temple of
God, claiming that he himself is God. . . . Then
the man of lawlessness will be revealed, whom
the Lord Jesus will consume with the breath of
his mouth and destroy by the splendor of his
coming.*

2 THESSALONIANS 2:3-4, 8

There is no shortage of people willing to
predict the future. In the late 1950s Jeane
Dixon predicted that the U.S. president
elected in 1960 would be assassinated
while in office. Her prediction was fulfilled
when John F. Kennedy was shot and killed
in Dallas, Texas, in November 1963. She
also predicted that a child born in the Middle East in 1962 would rise to prominence

in the 1980s, lead the world into an era without wars and suffering in the 1990s, and be recognized as a world leader by 1999. Obviously, Ms. Dixon didn't get them all right!

For the last thirty years some environmental scientists have predicted that growing world population, pollution, and depletion of the ozone layer would bring world disaster by the year 2000. While it is true that there are environmental problems, they fall well short of global disaster. In his book *The 1980's: Countdown to Armageddon,* Hal Lindsay wrote: "The decade of the 1980's could well be the last decade of history as we know it."[1] Both of these brilliant, sincere, and insightful people failed to predict the future with reliable accuracy.

Have you ever noticed how many people flock to theaters to see films such as *Silence of the Lambs, Natural Born Killers,* and *Independence Day?* It seems people have always been fascinated with the power of evil. The best-seller lists include titles of gruesome murder mysteries and grisly tales of psychotic and even supernatural evil. One company actually produced trading cards with the names, stories, and statistics of history's most famous serial killers.

No evil force has attracted more attention than the one Bible prophecies call the Antichrist. Even people who don't read or believe the Bible know that the number *666* is a symbol of demonic and hellish power.

> He [the Antichrist] required everyone—great and small, rich and poor, slave and free—to be given a mark on the right hand or on the forehead. And no one could buy or sell anything without that mark, which was either the name of the beast or the number representing his name. Wisdom is needed to understand this. Let the one who has understanding solve the number of the beast, for it is the number of a man. His number is 666. (Revelation 13:16-18)

## The Enemy

In the 1970s rock star Mick Jagger of the Rolling Stones recorded a song titled

"Sympathy for the Devil." Written from Satan's perspective, it describes his work in undermining a person's faith and also his involvement in activities surrounding Christ's crucifixion. While Mr. Jagger was certainly no theological giant, he did get some things right about our enemy. The Bible teaches that the origin of evil can be traced to the one we call Satan. Variously referred to as Lucifer, the devil, the father of lies, the deceiver, and the dragon (fourteen times in the book of Revelation), Satan was once an angel of great power and position whose pride caused him to rebel against God. Satan is now the great enemy of God, and he seeks to pervert and destroy all that God created as good. In the following passage, the prophet Isaiah is speaking about the corruption and evil of the pagan king of ancient Babylon as well as about Satan, whose malevolent influence lies behind all wickedness and sin.

> How you are fallen from heaven, O shining star, son of the morning! You have been thrown down to the earth,

you who destroyed the nations of the
world. For you said to yourself, "I will
ascend to heaven and set my throne
above God's stars. I will preside on the
mountain of the gods far away in the
north. I will climb to the highest heavens and be like the Most High." (Isaiah
14:12-14)

Satan was present in the Garden of Eden
in the form of the serpent, who tempted
Adam and Eve with the lie that they could
become like God. Three times in the wilderness Satan tempted Jesus to disobey or
disrespect his Father in heaven. And Satan
will mount his final assault on the authority and sovereignty of the Most High God
by raising up the figure of the Antichrist.

Throughout the centuries theologians
have debated, historians have speculated,
and preachers have pontificated about the
identity of the Antichrist. Timothy Weber
writes that in this century alone, those with
an interest in prophecy have used everything from contemporary world politics to
numerology in an attempt to discover the

identity of Antichrist.[2] In the mid-seventies the plot of the movie *The Omen* revolved around the Antichrist's being born as the son of the American ambassador to Great Britain. Well-meaning scholars have used complicated theories trying to prove that everyone from Hitler to Stalin to Mao Tse-tung to Saddam Hussein to Bill Gates and even to Prince Charles fits the Bible's description of the one whose number is 666.

Most of the Bible's references to the character of the Antichrist are found in the apocalyptic books of Daniel and Revelation. Apocalyptic literature is a form of religious writing that developed during times of intense persecution. When it was too dangerous to openly defy their tormentors, Jewish writers couched their message in writings characterized by bizarre images, dreams, visions, or conflicts between otherworldly creatures. These books are written in a style distinctly different from the rest of the Bible. Apocalyptic literature reads almost like a science-fiction story full of frightening descriptions of supernatural beasts, terrifying destruction, and weird symbolic numbers. In Revelation we see an apocalyptic description of the person of the Antichrist:

> The scarlet beast that was alive and then died is the eighth king. He is like the other seven, and he, too, will go to his doom. His ten horns are ten kings who have not yet risen to power; they will be appointed to their kingdoms for one brief moment to reign with the beast. They will all agree to give their power and authority to him. Together they will wage war against the Lamb, but the Lamb will defeat them because he is Lord over all lords and King over all kings, and his people are the called and chosen and faithful ones. (Revelation 17:11-14)

As we try to understand these portions of the Bible, we must remember that while apocalyptic writing conveys to us God's perfect truth, the writer never intended for the reader to interpret it in a strictly literal sense.

> Apocalyptic literature is very much like poetry in that it presents its truth differently than straight prose or historical narrative. . . . For example, we can learn a lot from the Book of Revelation's description of the Anti-Christ, but we're missing the mark if we think we have to insist that he will actually have "ten horns and seven heads, with ten crowns on his horns, and on each head a blasphemous name (Rev. 13:1).[3]

I would add that if the Antichrist were to match this description literally, he really wouldn't be that hard to identify!

The Bible teaches that Satan's ultimate challenge to God will be a person of tremendous power and malevolence who will seek to seduce the world and destroy God's people. In their Left Behind series of novels based on the biblical account of the end times, Tim LaHaye and Jerry B. Jenkins picture a scenario where a young, charismatic political leader gains enormous world influence by promising peace and prosperity. A century ago such influence would have been difficult, if not impossible, to imagine. Today, with global communication and economic networks linked by lightning-fast computers and code scanners, the possibility of control by information or economic domination is not so difficult to imagine.

Yet while we as Christians should be aware that our enemy is real and that we need to resist even the most charismatic leader who preaches or teaches contrary to God's revealed Word, our primary focus must be on the person and power of the one who came and is coming again—Jesus Christ.

## The King

As citizens of the United States, most of us are not too comfortable with the word *king*. After all, our last king was King George III of England in the eighteenth century. You may recall that our relationship with him didn't end on the most congenial terms. We tend to think of kings as either despotic tyrants, such as Saddam Hussein, or more or less figureheads, such as Prince Charles.

But when Jesus wears the title King of kings, it means something more glorious than we can begin to imagine.

> Then I saw heaven opened, and a white horse was standing there. And the one sitting on the horse was named Faithful and True. For he judges fairly and then goes to war. His eyes were bright like flames of fire, and on his head were many crowns. A name was written on him, and only he knew what it meant. He was clothed with a robe dipped in blood, and his title was the Word of God. . . . On his robe and thigh was written this title: King of kings and Lord of lords. (Revelation 19:11-16)

The Bible not only predicted the birth, death, and resurrection of Jesus, but it also clearly claims he will come again as a mighty king with unimaginable power and authority. The question on that day will not be, Who do you think the Antichrist is? but rather, Who is Jesus Christ, and how do you respond to him?

# The Accuracy of Bible Prophecy

As I mentioned earlier, living near Chicago has taught my family to pay attention to weather reports—especially in winter. A couple of times each year the weather stations will announce a winter storm warning. This usually means that the temperatures will plunge to ten, twenty, or even thirty degrees below zero, and snow is on the way. Although these forecasts are not 100 percent accurate, they are right often enough so that when we see the storm warning, we believe it and make appropriate preparations. When we take even a cursory look at Old Testament prophecy, we see that God has given us a trustworthy forecast of the future. In fact, God's forecast is even far more reliable than the best human predictions of the weather because he is always 100 percent accurate. Let's look at just one area of prophecy: prophecies concerning the coming of the Messiah into the world.

Seven hundred years before the birth of Christ, the prophet Micah predicted that a great king of Israel would be born in the lowly town of Bethlehem: "You, O Bethlehem Ephrathah, are only a small village in Judah. Yet a ruler of Israel will come from you, one whose origins are from the distant past. The people of Israel will be abandoned to their enemies until the time when the woman in labor gives birth to her son" (Micah 5:2-3). At about the same time, the prophet Isaiah predicted that a virgin would miraculously give birth to a child: "Look! The virgin will conceive a child! She will give birth to a son and will call him Immanuel—'God is with us'" (Isaiah 7:14). Notice that the prophecy even includes the name Immanuel, which was one of the names given to Jesus.

Roughly two hundred years later (and still five hundred years before Jesus' birth) the prophet Zechariah predicted that a great king would ride into Jerusalem on the back of a donkey: "Rejoice greatly, O people of Zion! Shout in triumph, O people of Jerusalem! Look, your king is coming to you. He is righteous and victorious, yet he is humble, riding on a donkey— even on a donkey's colt" (Zechariah 9:9).

Matthew 21:1-11 describes how Jesus ful-filled this prophecy when he rode into Jerusalem on a donkey, symbolizing his claim to the throne of David, on what we traditionally call Palm Sunday. Remember that Isaiah also prophesied *seven hundred years* beforehand that Jesus would be arrested, put on trial, beaten, flogged, and nailed to a Roman cross.

> He was despised and rejected—a man of sorrows, acquainted with bitterest grief. We turned our backs on him and looked the other way when he went by. He was despised, and we did not care. . . . He was beaten that we might have peace. He was whipped, and we were healed! All of us have strayed away like sheep. We have left God's paths to follow our own. Yet the Lord laid on him the guilt and sins of us all. (Isaiah 53:3-6)

Many see Psalm 16:10 as a prophetic indi-cation that the Messiah would not only suf-fer death but would also miraculously rise from the dead: "For you will not leave my soul among the dead or allow your godly one to rot in the grave." And Jesus prophesied his own resurrection in Matthew 12:40: "For as Jonah was in the belly of the great fish for three days and three nights, so I, the Son of Man, will be in the heart of the earth for three days and three nights."

Just how impressed should we be that Jesus fulfilled prophecies written centuries before his birth? In his book *The Next Move,* Rob Lindsted writes of a math professor named Dr. Peter Stoner, who calculated that the odds of a single person fulfilling just eleven of the clearest, most undisputed prophecies about Jesus Christ would be one in 1,000,000,000,000,000,000,000,000— that's one in one septillion! Dr. Lindsted suggests this would be like building a box with a volume of eighty cubic miles, filling it with dimes, and asking a blindfolded person to pick out one marked dime on the first try.[4] And this is taking into consideration only eleven specific prophecies. One scholar counted 109 Bible prophecies concerning Jesus' first coming, including twenty-seven that were fulfilled on a single day (the day of his crucifixion)![5] If God provided prophecy concerning Jesus' birth and death hundreds of years before those events occurred, we are compelled to ask, Why is all this so important to God, and why should we pay attention to it?

According to the Bible, Jesus is the key to the eternal destiny of every person who ever lived. Understanding the prophecies about Jesus is critical because Jesus was and is God's solution to the problem of human sin. God created us in his image to have an intimate, loving, and obedient relationship with him. Sin—a disregard for God's standard of purity and holiness—broke that relationship. Sin not only destroyed our relationship with God but also brought about physical death for every person as well as personal guilt, brokenness in human relationships, and spiritual death. Throughout the Old Testament, God instructed his people to seek forgiveness through the blood of sacrificial animals. While this seems barbaric to modern minds, God wanted to etch on our mind and heart the seriousness of sin and the importance of living rightly before a holy God. Ultimately, God fulfilled his own requirement for a perfect sacrifice by accomplishing once and for all what we could never accomplish for ourselves. In his infinite mercy and grace, he took on human flesh in the person of Jesus of Nazareth in order to become our sacrificial Lamb. In doing so, he fulfilled Isaiah's prophecy.

> And as a sheep is silent before the shearer, he did not open his mouth. From prison and trial they led him away to his death. But who among the people realized that he was dying for their sins—that he was suffering their punishment? He was oppressed and treated harshly, yet he never said a word. He was led as a lamb to the slaughter. (Isaiah 53:7-9)

Jesus is not just another interesting figure in ancient history. He is not just another face in the team photo of influential religious figures! He is the fulfillment of a mind-boggling series of prophecies: the very embodiment of the eternal God of the universe, the one who paid for our sin and brokenness by his own death and brings unquenchable hope of eternal life in heaven for those who believe. The Bible says this same Jesus lives today at the right hand of God the Father (Hebrews 10:12-13). But Bible prophecy tells us that before God executes the final act in the drama of salvation, before Christ's glorious appearing secures the final victory, there will be a great conflict between the King and his great enemy.

## The Conflict

In *Star Wars*—certainly one of the most popular motion pictures of all time—director George Lucas portrayed the classic conflict between good and evil. The villain, Darth Vader, was the very personification of evil. His black cape and ghastly black helmet gave him what we would imagine to be an almost demonic appearance. The forces of good were led by young hero Luke Skywalker and the wise old Jedi knight Ben (Obi-Wan) Kenobi. Perhaps one explanation for the film's enduring success is that we are all aware, at least on some level, that there is an ongoing war between good and evil, darkness and light, not only in the world around us but in our very soul. In his letter to the Ephesians, Paul describes the conflict between good and evil in this way:

> Put on all of God's armor so that you will be able to stand firm against all strategies and tricks of the Devil. For we are not fighting against people made of flesh and blood, but against the evil rulers and authorities of the unseen world, against those mighty powers of darkness who rule this world, and against wicked spirits in the heavenly realms. Use every piece of God's armor to resist the enemy in the time of evil, so that after the battle you will still be standing firm. (Ephesians 6:11-13)

The Bible can be seen as an epic account of the conflict between good and evil: a war between the one described as the enemy, Satan, and the sovereign and good God of the universe revealed to us in Jesus Christ. The conflict emerges in the very first pages of Genesis as Satan comes to Eve in the form of a serpent to distort the command of God through lies and deceit. The conflict continues through the history of the people of Israel, as God's people repeatedly give in to the temptations to follow after pagan deities and to ignore the commands of the one true God. Throughout this history, God uses his prophets to remind Israel of his truth and to warn of the consequences of disobedience.

We can see clearly the conflict between God and Satan when we look at the life of Jesus. The New Testament tells us that as Jesus prepared to begin his earthly ministry, Satan approached him with three tempta- tions designed to establish his own influ- ence over the Son of God. The last of the temptations reveals the scope of Satan's ambitions:

The Devil took him [Jesus] to the peak
of a very high mountain and showed
him the nations of the world and all
their glory. "I will give it all to you," he
said, "if you will only kneel down and
worship me."

"Get out of here, Satan," Jesus told
him. "For the Scriptures say,

'You must worship the Lord your God;
  serve only him.'" (Matthew 4:8-10)

And who among us cannot identify with
the words of the apostle Paul when he
describes the mighty struggle between
good and evil in our own heart?

I don't understand myself at all, for I
really want to do what is right, but I
don't do it. Instead, I do the very thing
I hate. . . . I know I am rotten through
and through so far as my old sinful
nature is concerned. No matter which
way I turn, I can't make myself do
right. . . . Oh, what a miserable person
I am! Who will free me from this life

that is dominated by sin? (Romans
7:15-18, 24)

This passage demonstrates that we are
each involved in a life-and-death struggle,
a battle over the spiritual condition of our
soul. The bad news is that without the
power of Christ, we will lose this battle.
But the good news is that because of Jesus'
death and resurrection, our victory is
guaranteed if we trust in him by faith. Paul
completes his thought by rejoicing and
saying: "Thank God! The answer is in Jesus
Christ our Lord. . . . So now there is no
condemnation for those who belong to
Christ Jesus. For the power of the life-
giving Spirit has freed you through Christ
Jesus from the power of sin that leads to
death" (Romans 7:25–8:2).

The conflict between the King of kings
and his archenemy, Satan, reaches its culmination in the prophecies of the book of
Revelation. In a series of spectacular and
horrifying apocalyptic visions, the apostle
John gives us a glimpse of the awesome—
and awful—final battle at the end of time:

"And they gathered all the rulers and their armies to a place called *Armageddon* in Hebrew" (Revelation 16:16).

The battlefield called Armageddon is actually a large plain in northern Israel, near the ancient city of Megiddo (southeast of the modern port of Haifa). Prophecy indicates that this strategic plain will be the focus of what could be called the last world war. Here the kings of the north, south, and east will join forces with the Antichrist to oppose God. Scripture indicates that at the culmination of that final battle, Christ will return to lead the armies of heaven in a great final victory over Satan and the Antichrist.

The Bible teaches that a great battle is raging in the spiritual world. Satan and his minions believe they can defeat God and destroy the world he created in love. Satan believes he can use temptation and sin to corrupt you and ultimately bring spiritual death to your soul and mine. But God has provided salvation through Jesus Christ for all who will believe. The prophecies of the

Bible tell us that Christ's victory over sin, death, and Satan is certain and that it will be sealed at the glorious second coming of the Lord.

# 3 Prophecy and Preparation:
## The Second Coming—Ready or Not?

*I can tell you this directly from the Lord: We who
are still living when the Lord returns will not
rise to meet him ahead of those who are in their
graves. For the Lord himself will come down from
heaven with a commanding shout, with the call
of the archangel, and with the trumpet call of
God. First, all the Christians who have died will
rise from their graves. Then, together with them,
we who are still alive and remain on the earth
will be caught up in the clouds to meet the Lord
in the air and remain with him forever. So comfort and encourage each other with these words.*

1 THESSALONIANS 4:15-18

In early January 1999 several members of
an extremist cult called Concerned Christians were arrested in Jerusalem for alleg-
edly planning a series of armed assaults on
Israeli police. Evidence suggests the cult
members hoped that their terrorist acts
would hasten the second coming of Christ.
The cult's leader, Monte Kim Miller,

described himself as a figure in the prophecies of Revelation and believed he was destined to die in the streets of Jerusalem in the last days of December 1999.

Although in recent years we have seen what seems to be an increase in cult activity, such fanaticism is not limited to the twentieth century. As early as the second century, the Montanist movement created controversy in the early church by attempting to predict the date of Jesus' return. In the early Middle Ages many scholars believed Jesus would return in the year 1000. They calculated that the year 1000 was the beginning of the sixth millennium of history (they set the creation at 4000 B.C.), and since God created the world in six days and a day is like a thousand years to him, it was logical to assume that his return would take place in the year 1000.

In the early 1840s many thousands of Americans believed that Baptist preacher William Miller, using something he called "millennial arithmetic," had accurately predicted the date of Christ's second coming as October 22, 1844. Some actually sold their farms, gave away their possessions, and let their fields go unharvested as they prepared themselves for Christ's arrival.[1] While we may find such stories somewhat amusing, we must at the same time respect the passion of such men and women to be ready for the return of their Lord and King!

## The King Is Coming!

When a father is returning from a long business trip, his children will wait up long past bedtime just for the thrill of welcoming him home. When a victorious athletic team returns to its home city after winning a world championship, throngs of fans crowd the airport terminal, anxious to share in the triumph. When a president or prime minister makes a visit to a town, the people literally "roll out the red carpet" in an effort to show honor and respect.

Bible prophecy tells us that Jesus, the King of kings and Lord of lords, will one day return to earth in great power and glory. What will that day be like? The Bible teaches four fundamental truths about the Second Coming:

## 1. Christ's Return Will Be Physical and Personal

The book of Acts tells us that when Jesus ascended into heaven after his resurrection, the disciples stood staring into the sky. Suddenly, two men robed in white stood with them, and said, "Men of Galilee, why are you standing here staring at the sky? Jesus has been taken away from you into heaven. And someday, just as you saw him go, he will return!" (1:11).

In 1942, during the darkest days of World War II in the Pacific theater, President Roosevelt commanded General Douglas MacArthur to retreat from the Philippine Islands before the U.S. troops had to surrender to the invading Japanese forces. MacArthur was not at all happy with this order, so as he left, he uttered some of the most famous words of the war. He said, "I shall return." History tells us that General MacArthur did return in 1944 to lead a series of brilliant victories that turned the tide of the war. When MacArthur promised to return, he did not mean he would return via telegram to inspire the troops;

he meant that he would actually return physically, in person, to lead them to triumph.

This is what Jesus means in the New Testament when he says in John 14:3, "When everything is ready, I will come and get you, so that you will always be with me where I am." This is what the book of Acts means when it promises, "Jesus has been taken away from you into heaven. And someday, just as you saw him go, he will return!" This is what Paul means when he writes, "The Lord himself will come down from heaven with a commanding shout" (1 Thessalonians 4:16). The personal return of Jesus is one of the most frequently mentioned events in the entire New Testament. One out of every twenty verses refers to his return, and it is mentioned in twenty-three of the twenty-seven books, in over three hundred separate references!

## 2. Christ's Return Will Be Public and Visible

"At last, the sign of the coming of the Son of Man will appear in the heavens, and there will be deep mourning among all the nations of the earth. And they will see the Son of Man arrive on the clouds of heaven with power and great glory" (Matthew 24:30).

People living a century ago would have considered it lunacy to claim that everyone in the world could witness a single event simultaneously. Yet in 1997 nearly half the world's population watched the funeral of Diana, princess of Wales, as it happened. If human beings can create computer and satellite technology capable of beaming dramatic images across the globe at the speed of light, imagine what the almighty Ruler of the universe can do!

Jesus said, "As the lightning lights up the entire sky, so it will be when the Son of Man comes" (Matthew 24:27). While we cannot begin to imagine the glory of God exploding into the earth's atmosphere, one thing is exceedingly clear: When Jesus returns, the world will notice!

## 3. Christ's Return Will Be Powerful

Every year newspapers carry terrifying reports of tropical storms and hurricanes wreaking havoc—particularly in the islands of the Caribbean. And despite advances in meteorological technology, human beings remain powerless in the face of such awesome forces. We may be able to predict the time of a hurricane's arrival onshore or measure the speed of its wind, but we can do nothing to prevent its coming. We can only make sure we are prepared.

When Christ came to earth the first time, he came in unexpected humility. In fact, most of the world completely missed the coming of the child who was laid in a lowly manger and raised as a carpenter's son. When Jesus rode into Jerusalem on what we now call Palm Sunday, he rode on the back of a donkey, thus fulfilling the prophecy of Zechariah 9:9: "Look, your king is coming to you. He is righteous and victorious, yet he is humble, riding on a donkey." Historians of ancient cultures tell us that when a king entered a city riding on a donkey, he was coming in peace. But if that same king rode on a white stallion, the people would tremble, for then the king was coming to lay waste and conquer.

It is this exact image of a conquering king that the Bible uses to describe Jesus' second coming: "Then I saw heaven opened, and a white horse was standing there. And the one sitting on the horse was named Faithful and True" (Revelation 19:11).

What will his power be like? Even those through whom God chose to communicate most intimately struggled to find the proper language and images to portray the awesome and shattering power of Christ's return. John describes it this way: "From his mouth came a sharp sword, and with it he struck down the nations. He ruled them with an iron rod, and he trod the winepress of the fierce wrath of almighty God. On his robe and thigh was written this title: King of kings and Lord of lords" (Revelation 19:15-16).

Like the coming of a hurricane, the second coming of Jesus Christ will be unimaginably powerful. We can say with certainty that he is coming (although we cannot predict the exact hour); we can prepare for his coming (by believing that his death saves us from the punishment our sins deserve), but we cannot keep him from coming nor fathom his power—power that makes the most terrible hurricane seem to be nothing more than a summer breeze.

> *The voice of the Lord echoes above the sea.*
> *The God of glory thunders.*
> *The Lord thunders over the mighty sea.*
> *The voice of the Lord is powerful;*
> *the voice of the Lord is full of majesty.*
> *The voice of the Lord splits the mighty cedars;*
> *the Lord shatters the cedars of Lebanon. . . .*
> *The voice of the Lord strikes with lightning bolts.*
> *The voice of the Lord makes the desert quake. . . .*
> *The voice of the Lord twists mighty oaks and strips the forests bare.*
> *In his Temple everyone shouts, "Glory!"*
> *(Psalm 29:3-9)*

## 4. Christ's Return Will Be Unexpected

My wife occasionally (although not often enough) has the opportunity to go away on a trip, leaving me alone with our four young children. As much as I hate to admit it, things very quickly get out of order: Dishes pile up in the sink, dirty clothes clog the hamper, and toys are strewn across the floor. Now if my wife has told me she will be home at 9:00 P.M., at 8:30 I spring into action. My behavior is definitely motivated by her imminent return. But what if she says, "I'll be back sometime tomorrow"? Now I don't plan to be ready just in the nick of time. I work to be *constantly prepared* for the moment when she walks through the door. Which is the purer form of motivation?

I have already mentioned the fact that many in the Christian world put forth a great deal of effort to use prophecy to predict the moment of Christ's return. That is fascinating because Jesus taught that not only would *we* not know the exact moment of his return, but also neither did *he* in his humanity: "However, no one knows the day or hour when these things will happen, not even the angels in heaven or the Son himself" (Mark 13:32).

When it came to discussions of his return, Jesus wanted to be very clear that we are not to be preoccupied with the date of his return but with the task of preparing for it. He made it quite clear that his return will take place when people least expect it.

> When the Son of Man returns, it will be like it was in Noah's day. In those days before the Flood, the people were enjoying banquets and parties and weddings right up to the time Noah entered his boat. People didn't realize what was going to happen until the Flood came and swept them all away. That is the way it will be when the Son of Man comes. (Matthew 24:37-39)

And in a letter to the Christians in Thessalonica, the apostle Paul wrote:

> You know quite well that the day of the Lord will come unexpectedly, like a thief in the night. When people are saying, "All is well; everything is peaceful and secure," then disaster will fall upon them as suddenly as a woman's

> birth pains begin when her child is about to be born. And there will be no escape. (1 Thessalonians 5:2-3)

Why would God choose to keep the date and time of such an event a secret? I think it's because he understands human nature. Most of us have a tendency to be motivated by deadlines. When a professor gives us three weeks to turn in a term paper, we wait until the third week to start writing it (or even the last night, as the case may be). If the government says taxes are due April 15, post offices are clogged on the night of April 14. And if God announced that Jesus would return at 8:05 A.M. on June 29, 2001, many of us would wait until the evening of June 28 before we got serious about our relationship with him. God does not want a faith coerced by a deadline. He wants our love, obedience, and trust anchored in his truth and faithfulness—whether he is coming tomorrow or a thousand years from tomorrow. God does not want us to wait until we *have* to be ready for Christ's coming; he wants us to live in a state of perpetual readiness for his coming. The issue, according to prophecy, is not *when* Jesus is coming, but the certainty *that he is* coming. The question is, are we ready—or not—for his return?

## Getting Ready

A bride typically begins preparing months in advance for her wedding day. She needs to order flowers and a wedding cake, select the music, choose dresses for her bridesmaids, and, most important, buy a beautiful white wedding gown and have it fitted. Such preparations are testimony to both the significance of a wedding and her love for her groom.

On several occasions the Bible refers to the church, consisting of all Christians— past, present, and future—as the bride of Christ: "'Let us be glad and rejoice and honor him. For the time has come for the wedding feast of the Lamb, and his bride has prepared herself. She is permitted to wear the finest white linen.' (Fine linen represents the good deeds done by the people of God)" (Revelation 19:7-8). What do we need to do to prepare for Christ's glorious return? Fortunately, the Bible offers very clear instructions:

*First, we must believe that Jesus Christ is the Son of God and that salvation is found only in him.* Jesus said, "I am the way, the truth, and the life. No one can come to the Father except through me" (John 14:6). When we believe that Jesus died on the cross to pay the penalty for our sin and that he rose from the dead to defeat forever the power of sin and death, we receive complete forgiveness of our sins and the guarantee of eternal life. The prophecies of Revelation symbolize the purity of forgiven believers by referring to their white garments and to the fact that their names are written in the Book of Life. The Bible is very clear: Only those whose sins have been forgiven in Christ are clothed in white and are listed forever in the Book of Life: "All who are victorious will be clothed in white. I will never erase their names from the Book of Life, but I will announce before my Father and his angels that they are mine" (Revelation 3:5). Farther along in the same book we read that "anyone whose name was not found recorded in the Book of Life was thrown into the lake of fire" (Revelation 20:15).

*Then, we must acknowledge our sin and ask God for forgiveness.* My great-grandfather on my mother's side was a crusty old mountain man the family called Grandpa Joe. I never had the honor of meeting Grandpa Joe personally, but through my mother's stories I know he lived a hard life as a coal miner in the hills of eastern Kentucky. Grandpa Joe's life was hard for plenty of other reasons as well. By all accounts he was not only a beloved grandfather but an alcoholic and an unrepentant philanderer, according to the stories they tell about him. When he would finally drag himself home after a month of carousing, he was prone to brag about his exploits—a source of shame and embarrassment for the family.

When Grandpa Joe lay dying from black lung, liver damage, and who knows what else, my mother, who was nineteen and a brand-new Christian, tried to reach out to him. She gently told him that Jesus died for our sins so we could go to heaven and that the Bible promises that if we confess our sins, God will forgive us. With one of his last breaths, Grandpa Joe made one of the saddest statements a person could ever make. "Daughter," he said, "I'd be a coward to ask for forgiveness now. I gotta take what's comin' to me."

In a way Grandpa Joe was right. He was going to meet a holy God, and he was going to get what was coming to him—just as we all are apart from the mercy of God through Jesus Christ. Where Grandpa Joe was wrong, of course, is that it is not cowardly to repent of sin and seek forgiveness. In fact, he was a coward *not* to make peace with God. How tragic to pass into eternity unprepared!

> Be dressed for service and well prepared, as though you were waiting for your master to return from the wedding feast. Then you will be ready to open the door and let him in the moment he arrives and knocks. . . . He may come in the middle of the night or

just before dawn. But whenever he
comes, there will be special favor for
his servants who are ready! (Luke
12:35-38)

Electricity is a marvelous power that
makes my life better in a thousand ways.
But if I want to repair a light switch in my
house, I would be foolish to just reach in
the wall and start handling those wires.
Without knowledge about how electricity
works and how to handle wires safely, I
would surely be shocked. If I grabbed even
one hot wire, my judgment would be swift
and sure. Now picture all the electrical
energy ever generated by all the nuclear
power plants in the world, and multiply
that by a billion. The light of God's holiness makes all that power look like a smol-
dering matchstick. The Bible teaches that
God's holiness cannot tolerate the presence of sin. Over and over again in the Old
Testament, God's anger at sin burned
forth and consumed both sin and sinner.
The Bible is equally clear that one day
each of us will stand before this holy God

to be judged. In what ways can we respond to that fact?

## *Four Responses*

*1. We can deny that God even exists.* The Bible says that even though God's existence can be discerned from all he has created, some refuse to acknowledge a being greater than themselves.

> God shows his anger from heaven against all sinful, wicked people who push the truth away from themselves. For the truth about God is known to them instinctively. God has put this knowledge in their hearts. From the time the world was created, people have seen the earth and sky and all that God made. They can clearly see his invisible qualities—his eternal power and divine nature. So they have no excuse whatsoever for not knowing God. (Romans 1:18-20)

To deny the existence of God is the height of human ignorance and arrogance. It would be like ants scurrying around on the sidewalk, refusing to believe human beings exist. To choose this option is to believe not only that the entire cosmos is an accident but also that all of the Bible's prophecies about Jesus Christ came true by chance and that following death there is nothing. As we read in the Psalms: "Only fools say in their hearts, 'There is no God'" (14:1).

*2. We can believe that God exists but that he is basically a sleepy old grandfather in the sky who doesn't really care all that much about how we live our life.* Research shows that three-quarters of all American adults strongly agree that there is only one true God, who created the world and rules over it today. Furthermore, more than nine out of ten believe in a god or gods that have power over the universe.[2] And yet, we look at our culture and see that these beliefs seem to make little difference in the way many people live their lives. In other words, people may believe that God exists, but that belief has no impact on their behavior. They ignore the power and holiness of the God of the Bible in favor of an impotent god who is benignly tolerant. This view disregards the concept of sin and re-creates "god" in *our* image, a god who simply wants us to do whatever makes us happy and would never presume to judge anyone.

> Yes, they knew God, but they wouldn't worship him as God or even give him thanks. And they began to think up foolish ideas of what God was like. The result was that their minds became dark and confused. Claiming to be wise, they became utter fools instead. And instead of worshiping the glorious, ever-living God, they worshiped idols made to look like mere people, or birds and animals and snakes. (Romans 1:21-23)

This approach assumes that the death of Jesus of Nazareth on a Roman cross was a meaningless waste of time. If the concept of sin is irrelevant and God is a tolerant being who does not judge, why would he give up his Son to atone for our sin?

*3. We can believe that God is holy and that we can hope to please him only by being "good enough."* In one survey, 56 percent of Americans polled strongly agreed that each of us has the power to determine our own spiritual destiny.[3] In other words, many believe that we earn our way to heaven by doing good things. But how good is good enough? Does God grade on a curve? Do you have to be "Mother Theresa good" or just "average-Joe good"? This mind-set is a modern version of the problem of legalism the New Testament church had to deal with. The Bible teaches that even "Mother Theresa good" isn't good enough. Romans 3:23 says that "all have sinned; all fall short of God's glorious standard." In other words, no one can ever be "good enough."

The Bible says that we are saved by God's grace, apart from anything good we try to do.

> God saved you by his special favor when you believed. And you can't take credit for this; it is a gift from God.

Salvation is not a reward for the good things we have done, so none of us can boast about it. For we are God's masterpiece. He has created us anew in Christ Jesus, so that we can do the good things he planned for us long ago. (Ephesians 2:8-10)

Let me be very clear. God wants us to be good and to do good things; it's just that those things do not save us—God does.

*4. We can take Jesus at his word.* This means we believe that when Jesus said, "I am the way, and the truth, and the life; no one comes to the Father but through me" (John 14:6, NASB), he was speaking the literal, absolute, and unalterable truth! It means that, just as we prepare carefully before we come into contact with electricity, so also we can approach a holy God only if we are adequately protected! Just as a nuclear engineer will don protective gear before handling radioactive material, we can come before God only if we are covered with the righteousness of Jesus Christ, since we cannot achieve perfect righteousness on our own. The Bible teaches that when we acknowledge and confess our sin and ask Christ to forgive us on the basis of his death on the cross, we are completely forgiven. From that point forward we are "clothed" with Christ in the eyes of God, and Christ's righteousness covers our sin. This is the gospel, the almost unfathomable Good News, that on the day when we stand before God in judgment, he will see, not the stains of our sin and failure, but the pure and spotless garment of the righteousness of Jesus Christ that covers us completely. He will take us to spend eternity in heaven with him in the place he has prepared for us!

# 4 Prophecy and Eternity:
## Heaven—My Father's House

*Don't be troubled. You trust God, now trust in
me. There are many rooms in my Father's home,
and I am going to prepare a place for you. If
this were not so, I would tell you plainly. When
everything is ready, I will come and get you, so
that you will always be with me where I am.*

JOHN 14:1-3

My second son, Jesse, has always had a
fascination with whales. In fact, it's more
than a fascination—he adores whales. He
collects plastic whale figures of all types:
humpbacks, belugas, sperm whales, nar-
whals—he loves them all. But he especially
loves killer whales. He must have ten books
on killer whales alone, and for several
years he slept with a stuffed killer whale in
his bed. So imagine his excitement when
we finally visited Sea World in Aurora,
Ohio, and he saw Shamu, a real live killer
whale! When we arrived at the park and he
peered into the giant tank and caught his

first glimpse of the huge, glistening black-and-white creature, his eyes grew as big as saucers, and he said in an awestruck whisper, "Dad, it's really *big!*"

Now, what if, when I had suggested the trip, he had responded, "No thanks, Dad. I'd rather just stay home and play with my plastic whales"? Unfortunately, that's exactly the way many of us think about heaven! We know it's there, but we are not all that interested and would prefer to settle for the pale imitation that is this life. Consider this quote from David Van Biema, who wrote a cover story for *Time* magazine entitled, "Does Heaven Exist?"

> Practicing Christians believe heaven is our destination and reward, reunion with those we love, our real home, our permanent address. It is the New Jerusalem and the communion of the saints, the eternal Eucharist, the everlasting Easter and a million Christmases. It is the eternal, ongoing, ever growing experience of God—the ecstatic dream of St. John, "Holy, holy,

holy!" And yet, in a curious way, heaven is AWOL. People still believe in heaven, it's just that their concept of what it is has grown foggier and they hear about it much less frequently from their pastors.[1]

## Is Heaven Real?

Of all the questions we find ourselves asking about the end times—When will the world end? When will the Antichrist appear? When and how will Jesus return?—perhaps the most intriguing are those about heaven. The place to begin is to ask, Is heaven real, or is it just a pie-in-the-sky religious fantasy? We can respond to this question in two ways:

*1. We can believe that heaven is not a real, literal place and is, therefore, either an escapist fantasy or a theoretical principle.* In this view, shared by Sigmund Freud, Karl Marx, and many others, heaven is something human beings dreamed up to make themselves feel better when faced with the reality of death. To take this view makes Jesus a liar, for he clearly promised his disciples that he would both prepare a place for them in heaven and come to take them to be with him forever: "There are many rooms in my Father's home, and I am going to prepare a place for you. If this were not so, I would tell you plainly. When everything is ready, I will come and get you, so that you will always be with me where I am" (John 14:3-4).

During his own crucifixion, Jesus also promised heaven to the thief dying by his side: "I assure you, today you will be with me in paradise" (Luke 23:43). To believe that heaven is simply some kind of psychological crutch flies in the face of what the Bible claims Jesus said, and it also discounts the common longing of countless people in every culture and religion for an experience of love and joy after death. C. S. Lewis suggested that it would be strange indeed for a species to be created with the physiological drive of hunger without nature's offering the corresponding possibility of food. In the same way, he says, it is unimaginable that human beings were created with a spiritual hunger for heaven without a corresponding possibility of the fulfillment of that longing: "If I find in myself a desire which no experience in this world can satisfy, the most probable explanation is that I was made for another world."[2]

The Bible would agree that you and I have been created for another world. The ancient writer of Ecclesiastes says it this way: "[God] has planted eternity in the human heart" (Ecclesiastes 3:11).

*2. We can believe that heaven is the real world, for which this life is only a kind of dress rehearsal.* The more we study and understand what the Bible teaches, the more clearly we see that heaven is not presented as a dreamlike otherworld but rather as a stunningly beautiful place that makes this earthly existence seem nothing more than a dim, shadowy preface. This seems backward to us only because we are conditioned by our modern prejudice toward materialism. We are taught that what can be measured, photographed, and dissected is more real than what is intangible, unseen, or spiritual. But we all know better. Let me ask you, Which is more real—the chair on which you are sitting, or the relationship, good or bad, you have (had) with your mother? Which is more real—the concrete, wood, and nails of your house, or the love or conflict that exists within it? In his brilliant essay *The Great Divorce,* C. S. Lewis suggests that heaven is so real that were we to enter it as we are now, we would be unable even to pick a daisy, for even a flower would be too heavy for us to lift. The reality of heaven is so bright and solid that it would make our earthly existence seem unreal, insignificant, and colorless by comparison.[3]

## Where Is Heaven?

It was not long after he said this that he was taken up into the sky while they were watching, and he disappeared into a cloud. As they were straining their eyes to see him, two white-robed men suddenly stood there among them.

They said, "Men of Galilee, why are you standing here staring at the sky? Jesus has been taken away from you into heaven. And someday, just as you saw him go, he will return!" (Acts 1:9-11)

In 1961 Russian cosmonaut Yury Gagarin became the first man in space. Upon his return to earth, he earned points with the atheistic communist regime by proclaiming that he hadn't seen God. Astronomers tell us that the sun is just one of a *million million* stars in the Earth's galaxy, the Milky Way. And the Milky Way is just one of *twenty* galaxies that make up what is known as a "cluster." And then there are superclusters consisting of tens of thousands of galaxies, some of which stretch across more than a half billion light-years of space.[4] Yet Mr. Gagarin traveled a mere one hundred miles from Earth and concluded that God did not exist. That's somewhat like sticking your foot in the Pacific Ocean and concluding that whales do not exist because one didn't bite your big toe! So if heaven is real, where is it? What are the possible answers to this question?

*1. Heaven is on earth.* This is the view of progressive utopianism, prevalent at the beginning of the twentieth century. It is the belief that if human governments and institutions can create enough jobs, prosperity, and scientific breakthroughs, civilization will progress steadily until heaven comes to pass on earth. Even though two devastating world wars have dampened such optimism, many in affluent North America would agree with evangelical scholar David Wells when he says, "It's difficult for some people to conceive of anything that is really much better than this life. Sure, they're going to be appalled by the eleven o'clock news. But those buddies on the beer commercial saying, 'It doesn't get much better than this' are speaking more deeply than they realize." [5]

If it is indeed true that there's nothing better than this life, then the apostle Paul is right: "If we have hope in Christ only for this life, we are the most miserable people in the world" (1 Corinthians 15:19).

Peter Kreeft, author of *Everything You*

*Ever Wanted to Know about Heaven—But
Never Dreamed of Asking,* writes:

> We moderns have lost much of medieval
> Christendom's *faith* in Heaven because
> we have lost its *hope* of Heaven, and we
> have lost its *hope* of Heaven because we
> have lost its *love* of Heaven. And we have
> lost its *love* of Heaven because we have
> lost its sense of Heavenly glory. . . . Our
> pictures of Heaven are dull, platitudi-
> nous and syrupy; therefore so is our
> faith, our hope, and our love of Heaven.[6]

*2. Heaven is in us.* In this view, held by
many who embrace New Age philosophies,
heaven is an internal state of perfect
peace, personal fulfillment, and oneness
with the cosmos, achieved by relaxation,
meditation, or reading enough self-help
books. This view, which is totally foreign to
what the Bible teaches, reduces heaven to
something subjective that we find in ourselves or create for ourselves.

*3. Heaven is a real place where God dwells in
the fullness of his power and glory.*

> As I looked, I saw a door standing open
> in heaven, . . . and I saw a throne in
> heaven and someone sitting on it! The
> one sitting on the throne was as bril-
> liant as gemstones—jasper and carne-
> lian. And the glow of an emerald
> circled his throne like a rainbow.
> Twenty-four thrones surrounded him,
> and twenty-four elders sat on them. . . .
> And from the throne came flashes of
> lightning and the rumble of thun-
> der. . . . In front of the throne was a
> shiny sea of glass, sparkling like crystal.
> (Revelation 4:1-6)

In Isaiah 66:1, God says, "Heaven is my
throne, and the earth is my footstool."
This means that God does not inhabit
space in the way we know it. God is spirit,
but he is also exceedingly real. We see an
example of this in the resurrected body
of Jesus. He was real enough to eat fish
and be touched by Thomas but spiritual
enough to walk through locked doors and
transport himself instantaneously from
one physical location to another. In the

same way, heaven is a spiritual place, yet a very real place. But heaven is not a location in physical space, like Topeka, Kansas, or the planet Neptune. And although one can argue that the "new heaven and new earth" of Revelation indicates that the glories of heaven may, in fact, include the perfection of this tired planet, at the present time heaven occupies a spiritual space infinitely larger and more mind-boggling than any supernova or exploding galaxy. C. S. Lewis suggests that, by comparison, heaven would make the physical universe—in all its vastness—seem as if it were indoors.[7]

When Jesus said, "I go to prepare a place for you," he was talking about a place altogether different from our physical universe but most definitely real.

## What Will Heaven Be Like?

It happens to almost all of us sooner or later. It is a moment we look forward to—and dread. Within months of writing this sentence, it will happen to me. I will receive an unsettling and disturbing piece of mail. It won't be a notice of an IRS audit (at least I hope not); it won't be a summons to jury duty or even an invitation to receive a "free" gift if only I'll sit through a sales pitch for a time-share condo in Katmandu or Key West. No, it will be an invitation to my twenty-fifth high school class reunion.

That reunion is disturbing because it is a kind of mile marker in life, pointing out the astonishing passage of time. It tells me I've been out of high school for a quarter of a century, *one-fortieth of a millennium!* I'm now the same age my father was when I graduated—and I thought he was a fossil then! It is unsettling because when I attend this reunion, I will be seeing people who, in my memory, have not aged a single day, and they will be seeing me (it's hard to tell which is more frightening). It means feeling the need to say, "You haven't changed a bit!" when I really want to say, "My goodness, what happened to your face?" I find myself wondering, *Who will be there? Will I recognize them? Will they recognize me? Will I even remember their names?* I think that, if we are honest, many of us wonder these same things about heaven.

## *Will We Know Each Other in Heaven?*

From the beginning of God's relationship with humanity, names have been important. God tells Moses his name (Exodus 3:14-15) and assures him that he knows Moses by name (verse 4). Throughout the Bible, names imply personhood and relationship. Several times in the book of Revelation the apostle John mentions the Book of Life in which are inscribed all the names of the redeemed. This strongly implies that, although heaven will be unimaginably different from this earthly life, there will be a sense of personhood and relationship. In Matthew 22:30 Jesus was careful to point out that marriage, as we know it, will not exist in heaven. We can only guess that this is because we will no longer need physical intimacy. Yet there is every indication that we will not be nameless, faceless cherubs floating in the cosmos but, rather, the same distinct beings but with new spiritual bodies, able to recognize and know each other.

Our earthly bodies, which die and
decay, will be different when they are
resurrected, for they will never die.
Our bodies now disappoint us, but
when they are raised, they will be full
of glory. They are weak now, but when
they are raised, they will be full of
power. They are natural human bodies
now, but when they are raised, they will
be spiritual bodies. For just as there are
natural bodies, so also there are spiritual bodies. (1 Corinthians 15:42-44)

## Will Heaven Be Boring?

It is a scene that I suspect repeats itself millions of times in homes all across America.
If you've ever had children who are out of
school for the summer, my guess is that it
has happened in your home, too. My
seven-year-old comes downstairs at 6:05
A.M. with sleep still in his eyes and a full
day of the endless possibilities of child-
hood lying open before him—no school,
no work, no responsibilities (other than to
make his bed and pick up his toys). Yet he
heaves a great sigh and complains with

world-weary conviction and a straight face, "Dad, there's nothing to do." This, mind you, with TV, VCR, and enough sports equipment and art supplies to keep both Michael Jordan and Michaelangelo busy for a month. "I'm bored," he says.

We become bored when we experience life as being monotonous or unchanging for an extended period of time (in my son's case, about thirty-five seconds). Things that take a long time can be boring. Things that don't change can be boring. So when we use the phrase *eternal life* to describe the hope and reality of heaven, is it any wonder that we also find ourselves asking, Will heaven be boring? What will we do for all eternity?

There is a great deal about heaven that we do not know, nor could we comprehend it even if God were to send us a blueprint. But I think we can say with great certainty that heaven will be anything but boring! Heaven will not only be a joyous encounter with our risen Lord Jesus Christ and a glad reunion with loved ones who have passed on before, but it will also be a ceaseless adventure in a new kind of worship and a new kind of life.

## The Adventure of Worship

Having been raised in a pastor's family and then becoming a pastor myself, I have participated in somewhere around three thousand worship services. As boys, my brothers and I were in church every time the doors were open—Sunday morning, Sunday night, Wednesday night—and many times when they were not! I remember when I was a boy, it seemed that we sang through the entire hymnal every Sunday evening. All that singing, plus what seemed to be a two-hour sermon (I'm sure Dad's messages were outstanding, but by seven thirty my ten-year-old brain had checked out!), gave me a pretty good understanding of the phrase *eternal worship*. I remember wondering to myself, with more than a little dread, *Is this really what heaven is going to be like?*

Although worship will be one of our primary activities in heaven, and even though we will worship for all eternity, we will never be bored. Why? *First, because our worship will be thrilling!* The Bible compares heavenly worship to "what sounded like the shout of a huge crowd, or the roar of mighty ocean waves, or the crash of loud thunder" (Revelation 19:6).

If you've ever attended a college football game with one hundred thousand people cheering, you know that can be pretty exciting. Now multiply that experience by a billion or so, for the Bible says that one day all Christians who have ever lived—from every nation and tongue—will lift their voices in praise! I don't think any of us will have trouble staying awake, do you?

*Second, and even more important, the God we worship is of such infinite and ever changing beauty that we will never exhaust our desire to see and learn more of him.* Psalm 27:4 says: "The one thing I ask of the Lord—the thing I seek most—is to live in the house of the Lord all the days of my life, delighting in the Lord's perfections and meditating in his Temple." Consider this description of worship in heaven:

After this, I heard the sound of a vast crowd in heaven shouting, "Hallelujah! Salvation is from our God. Glory and power belong to him alone." . . . Then the twenty-four elders and the four living beings fell down and worshiped God, who was sitting on the throne. They cried out, "Amen! Hallelujah!" And from the throne came a voice that said, "Praise our God, all his servants, from the least to the greatest, all who fear him." Then I heard again what sounded like the shout of a huge crowd, or the roar of mighty ocean waves, or the crash of loud thunder: "Hallelujah! For the Lord our God, the Almighty, reigns." (Revelation 19:1-6)

*Third, the reason we will never grow bored has to do with how we think of eternity. Contrary to my experience in church as a child, eternity is not the endless passage of time—it is the absence of time.* Eternity is the great "forever now"—past, present, and future all rolled up into the fullness of the moment. Even now in our earthbound existence we sometimes catch a glimpse of the eternal now. When we are so caught up in a glorious sunset or the beauty of a loved one's face or the miraculous birth of a child that we lose track of time altogether—heaven is that moment, and it is never boring.

*Finally, heaven will not be boring because we will worship and obey God with all that we are—our whole being.* Psalm 103:1 says: "Praise the Lord, O my soul; all my inmost being, praise his holy name (NIV). Our present worship and obedience are partial at best. We are distracted, halfhearted, on-again, off-again, because we see God's glory dimly and because we are fallen creatures who live in a fallen world. But then, in heaven, we shall see him face-to-face, and we will worship with all that is within us. Stop for a moment, and think of some activity that has involved the totality of your being—your mind, your body, your emotions—all that you are. My guess is that whatever came to your mind—perhaps playing a musical instrument comes closest—brought a fulfillment, joy, and delight unmatched by any other human experience. Our worhip in heaven will be like that.

## Ruling with Our King

Walk into any Christian bookstore or religious gift shop in America, and you will find shelves full of pudgy little winged figurines with impossibly cute expressions on their cherubic faces. While these are simply some artist's childlike view of angels, they have become for some a kind of theology of heaven. When some people think of heaven, they assume that when they die, they will become angels, with wings and halos. The Bible teaches that, on the contrary, angels and people are two completely distinct kinds of created beings, and we should not mistake one for the other. Although the Bible indicates that believers will be resurrected with new spiritual bodies, it never says that we will become angels! In fact, the Bible seems to indicate that with our resurrected spiritual bodies we will be more like warriors than cherubs. Rather than spending eternity strumming harps and floating on clouds, we will be ruling a vast kingdom under the command of our glorious King. Now, I admit, I have no idea what sort of duty this might entail, but my hunch is that it won't be pushing paper or collating end-of-the-millennium reports!

In the book of Matthew, Jesus gives us a hint as to the eternal assignment he has in mind for his followers. He promises that those who have invested themselves boldly in the kingdom, by faith, will one day hear God say, "Well done, my good and faithful servant. You have been faithful in handling this small amount, so now I will give you many more responsibilities. Let's celebrate together!" (Matthew 25:21).

Could it be that Jesus is even now preparing not only a place for us in heaven but also a unique responsibility, a way for us to serve our King for all eternity? Could it be that when the Bible speaks about the crowns people receive in heaven, it is not merely using symbolism? The New Testament seems to use the image of a crown to signify both a reward for a task well done (for example,

1 Corinthians 9:24 mentions a reward that an athlete receives for winning a race) and a sign of authority to rule. The New Testament mentions at least four specific crowns:

1. *The crown of righteousness:* The apostle Paul refers to this crown in 2 Timothy 4:8. It seems to be a reward for those who, like Paul himself, have served faithfully in ministry, motivated by the certainty of Christ's second coming.

2. *The crown of life:* James tells us that those who have endured severe trials or persecution will receive this crown (James 1:12). Revelation 2:10 echoes James's words: "Don't be afraid of what you are about to suffer. . . . Remain faithful even when facing death, and I will give you the crown of life."

3. *The crown of rejoicing:* Paul says that those who came to faith in Christ as a result of his evangelistic efforts are his crown, his cause for rejoicing (1 Thessalonians 2:19). And Jesus

said that when even one sinner repents, there is rejoicing in heaven (Luke 15:10).

4. *The crown of glory:* The apostle Peter refers to this in 1 Peter 5:4. Some see in Peter's use of the title Chief Shepherd an indication that this crown is reserved for those who have served as shepherds, pastors, elders, and spiritual leaders of the church on earth. Perhaps this crown will designate those who will share leadership with the Lord in heaven.

Now, clearly, all believers will share in the life, joy, righteousness, and glory of heaven. But the mention of these specific crowns seems to indicate that there is some correlation, however mysterious to our human understanding, between faithful service in this life and the responsibilities and privileges of heaven.

In his book *One Minute after You Die,* Dr. Erwin Lutzer suggests that when Jesus says, "You were faithful with a few things, I will put you in charge of many things" (Mat-

thew 25:23, NASB), he perhaps meant that
he will assign us responsibilities commen-
surate with the faithfulness we displayed
here on earth.[8]

Remember my son's toy whales at the
beginning of this chapter? While those toy
whales were only the faintest representa-
tion of the power and beauty of Shamu, my
son's *love* and *knowledge* of whales prepared
him for and heightened his enjoyment of
the real thing when he finally experienced
it. In the same way, growing in our love
and knowledge of Christ now will prepare
us to enjoy heaven when we finally get
there and see Jesus face-to-face.

# 5 Going Home!

*I heard a loud shout from the throne, saying, "Look, the home of God is now among his people! He will live with them, and they will be his people. God himself will be with them. He will remove all of their sorrows, and there will be no more death or sorrow or crying or pain. For the old world and its evils are gone forever."*

REVELATION 21:3-4

A few years ago my wife and I took our three young sons (now there are four) on a trip to Malaysia to visit relatives. It was a wonderful adventure. Besides seeing my wife's aunts and uncles whom she hadn't seen in many years, we were able to visit her birthplace and the international school she attended while her parents served as missionaries. We toured two of the great cities of the world, Kuala Lumpur and Singapore. Our boys particularly enjoyed our visit to the fabulous Singapore Zoo! But after two weeks of living out of suitcases, it was time to go home.

The return trip involved several flights and a total of twenty hours of travel. Have you ever traveled for twenty hours with three children under the age of six? Like the concept of dog years, traveling with children on an airplane changes one's experience of time. The boys were hungry at times when no food was available; they were wide awake when we needed them to sleep; one was sick with a virus he'd picked up along the way; and there was no extra seat for our ten-month-old baby, so one of us had to hold him the entire way. It wasn't long before the inevitable questions started: "How much longer, Daddy?" "Are we there yet?" "When are we going to get there?" And when a pitiful little voice would plead, "I just want to go home," my wife would pat me on the head and say, "Just be patient, honey. It won't be long."

When we begin to contemplate heaven, we can feel a bit the same way. We know the destination; we have a deep longing for our eternal home. But we wonder, *How long until we get there, and what do we do in the meantime?* Heaven may be real and more exciting than we can ever imagine, and our new spiritual bodies may be pain free and glorious, but how does that help us now?

## Prophecy As a Warning and an Encouragement

The Bible gives strong evidence that the earliest Christians asked similar questions. They had come to faith in Christ, but they were facing terrible suffering, and some of their friends and loved ones had already died. They began to wonder, *When will our suffering end? How much longer? Is it really worth it?* Peter wrote a letter to encourage believers who were going through intense persecution. He reminds these young Christians that although they may experience trials in this life, the hope of the promised glory of the next life will sustain and strengthen them in their suffering.

> These trials are only to test your faith, to show that it is strong and pure. It is being tested as fire tests and purifies gold—and your faith is far more precious to God than mere gold. So if your

faith remains strong after being tried
by fiery trials, it will bring you much
praise and glory and honor on the day
when Jesus Christ is revealed to the
whole world. You love him even
though you have never seen him.
Though you do not see him, you trust
him; and even now you are happy with
a glorious, inexpressible joy. Your
reward for trusting him will be the
salvation of your souls. (1 Peter 1:7-9)

In the same way that the promise of
heaven encouraged those early believers,
an understanding of prophecy can both
prepare us for the life to come and sustain
us with hope and joy during this life with
all its struggles. How does an understanding of prophecy about heaven do that?

*The prophecies about heaven warn us to be
prepared for the inevitable coming of God's
judgment.* The need to be prepared is a
repeated theme in the teaching of Jesus:

The coming of the Son of Man can be
compared with that of a man who left

home to go on a trip. He gave each of his employees instructions about the work they were to do, and he told the gatekeeper to watch for his return. So keep a sharp lookout! For you do not know when the homeowner will return—at evening, midnight, early dawn, or late daybreak. Don't let him find you sleeping when he arrives without warning. What I say to you I say to everyone: Watch for his return! (Mark 13:34-37)

The first and most important step in being prepared is to receive Jesus Christ as Savior and Lord. The writer of the Gospel of John wrote: "But these [accounts of Jesus' miracles] are written so that you may believe that Jesus is the Messiah, the Son of God, and that by believing in him you will have life" (John 20:31).

If you have already received Christ as Savior by faith and have committed yourself to serving and obeying him as Lord, there is still much to do to prepare yourself for his coming! Everything we do can be seen as a preparation for that day. Our earthly worship prepares us for our worship around the heavenly throne; our service to others prepares us for the service we will render the King of heaven; our faithfulness in building his kingdom on earth prepares us to reign with him in the eternal kingdom of heaven.

*The prophecies about heaven offer Christians a rock-solid hope that sustains them in the face of death and suffering.* One of the great themes of the Bible is redemption. To redeem means to exchange something of lesser value for something of greater value. As a child you may have experienced the power of redemption on a small scale by collecting aluminum cans and redeeming them for money. On a much greater scale, the New Testament teaches that Jesus redeemed us when he paid the price demanded for our sin by shedding his blood on the cross: "He is so rich in kindness that he purchased our freedom through the blood of his Son, and our sins are forgiven" (Ephesians 1:7).

The Bible also tells us that at his glorious

second coming or at the moment of our death, Christ will receive us into heaven and exchange our sufferings for glory. Therefore, we have a hope that sustains us.

> Yet what we suffer now is nothing compared to the glory he will give us later. . . . All creation anticipates the day when it will join God's children in glorious freedom from death and decay. For we know that all creation has been groaning as in the pains of childbirth right up to the present time. And even we Christians, although we have the Holy Spirit within us as a fore-taste of future glory, also groan to be released from pain and suffering. We, too, wait anxiously for that day when God will give us our full rights as his children, including the new bodies he has promised us. (Romans 8:18-23)

*The prophecies about heaven inspire us to greater obedience.* A couple of years ago I went to see our family doctor for a physical examination. Although I had promised

both my wife and my mother that I would
have a checkup when I turned forty, I
had procrastinated until about two weeks
before my forty-first birthday. But as soon
as I had set the appointment, during which
I knew I would not only see my doctor
face-to-face but have my weight and cholesterol checked, I noticed something interesting. Some of my habits, my day-to-day
behavior, started to change. Fruit replaced
chips as a snack; salad replaced burger and
fries at lunch; I exercised with a bit more
determination. In short, I began to prepare for my physical. In the same way,
when we are convinced of the truth of
Bible prophecy—that each of us has an
"appointment" with almighty God, who
will sit in judgment over us; that heaven
is real; and that Jesus is really going to
return— then we desire nothing more
than to be fully prepared for that time.
Paul tells the Colossians:

> Since you have been raised to new life
> with Christ, set your sights on the reali-
> ties of heaven, where Christ sits at

God's right hand in the place of honor
and power. Let heaven fill your
thoughts. Do not think only about
things down here on earth. For you
died when Christ died, and your real
life is hidden with Christ in God. And
when Christ, who is your real life, is
revealed to the whole world, you will
share in all his glory. (Colossians 3:1-4)

From our human perspective, we typically assume that the past and the present
determine the future. Notice that here
Paul reverses that thinking by suggesting
that it is our awareness of the future, not
the past, that determines our current atti-
tudes and actions. Prophecy operates on
the idea that having a knowledge about the
future has the power to influence the present! The prophecies of the Bible tell us
what is going to happen. The appointment
is set. We are going to meet the Lord
face-to-face. The question is whether or
not we will be prepared. What *will be*
should affect what we are and do now.
Who we *shall be* in Christ should determine

who we are and how we live right now as believers.

*The prophecies about heaven encourage us to be living witnesses.* Josh McDowell tells the story of a corporate headhunter who had a unique strategy for revealing the character qualities of any prospective executive. He would welcome the candidate into his office, disarm him or her with the offer of a beverage, prop his feet up on the desk, and very casually talk about sports or family until he was sure the person was relaxed. Then he would surprise the candidate with, "So what's your purpose in life?" He found that most were prepared to talk about business, management style, or corporate objectives but not about the purpose of their life. That is, until he asked the question of one man who responded without hesitation, "My purpose is to go to heaven when I die and to take as many people with me as I can."[1]

How would you respond to the same question? If the prophecies we have examined in this book are true—if Jesus is coming again, if one day every human being will stand to be judged by a holy God, if the only way to be prepared for that day is through the mercy of Jesus Christ—then every Christian has both the responsibility and the privilege of sharing the Good News with as many people as possible.

*The prophecies about heaven create joy in the life of the Christian.* For several summers my extended family gathered at the lake cottage of some church friends to spend a few days together. Before we headed up to the cottage, these friends advised us to get our drinking water from "the spring." So we went with some curiosity one day to find this spring. Following the directions, we came to a small, out-of-the-way place on the side of the road just big enough to park a car, where a pipe was poking out of the ground. There was no spigot, nothing to catch the water; it just gushed out of the pipe onto the ground. Then I saw a small plaque by the pipe that read something like this: "A local farmer dug this well by hand to find water for his cattle. He struck an artesian spring, and water has been flowing at the rate of forty gallons a minute since 1890." I had to stop to let that sink in. That pipe gushed forty gallons a minute, twenty-four hundred gallons an hour, almost sixty thousand gallons a day of the coldest, purest water you've ever tasted. And it had been doing so for over a hundred years—absolutely free! All we had to do was hold a bucket under the water and take some home.

Jesus said, "If you only knew the gift God has for you and who I am, you would ask me, and I would give you living water. . . . It becomes a perpetual spring within [you], giving [you] eternal life" (John 4:10, 14).

In his book *Everything You Ever Wanted to Know about Heaven—but Never Dreamed of Asking,* Peter Kreeft writes, "Joy bubbles and brims at the heart of God. . . . God is an overflowing fountain of joy, a volcanic explosion of joy, a trillion burning suns of joy, a joy that would utterly break our hearts if we touched even a drop of it at its source."[2]

*The prophecies about heaven give a sense of unquenchable hope.* In the midst of the most crushing emotional or physical pain and anguish, the prophecies about heaven comfort us with the hope of something better.

> Yet what we suffer now is nothing compared to the glory he will give us later. For all creation is waiting eagerly for that future day when God will reveal who his children really are. . . . Now that we are saved, we eagerly look forward to this freedom. For if you already have something, you don't need to hope for it. But if we look forward to something we don't have yet, we must wait patiently and confidently. (Romans 8:18-25)

In July 1988 our family received the crushing news that my youngest brother, John, a twenty-year-old college student, had been killed in a traffic accident. As anyone who has walked that dark valley knows, there are no words to describe the shock and pain. Even though the members of my entire family are committed Christians—my father and other brother are also pastors—and we knew that John knew Christ and was now in the presence of his Lord, and though our grief was permeated with hope, we grieved nonetheless. Although I had the hope of heaven, for me it was more an academic hope than a personal hope, for I had never really given heaven much thought up to that point.

Sometime in the year that followed his death, I had a dream about my late brother. I know we all dream every night and that our dreams are generated by a complex combination of waking experiences and subconscious fears and desires. But this was one of those exceedingly powerful dreams that leave you wondering whether it was a dream or an actual event. It was one of those dreams—if it was a dream—that was, perhaps, more real than the world we inhabit in our waking hours.

I dreamed that my brother came back to us. In my dream people who died in tragic accidents had the opportunity to return to spend one full day with their loved ones. At the end of that twenty-four-hour period, John had to decide whether to stay on earth and live the rest of his life as it would have been or to return to heaven and wait for us to join him. We had a wonderful day. We hugged and laughed and told stories the way we always did—only with greater joy. But as the hour approached for his decision, John grew more pensive. He began to talk about heaven, and his voice and face began to take on qualities that were—well, more than John. I cannot recall what he said about heaven except that as he spoke, his face radiated a kind of joy and longing I had never seen before. As he spoke, we knew he loved us enough to want to stay just for our sake, but we also knew that if we allowed him to choose, he would return to where he longed to be.

When he finished talking, we sat in silence for a long time as the sun went down outside the window. Then one of us said, "It's OK, big guy. We'll be there soon." We all hugged again, and he was gone.

I know it was just a dream. But since that dream, heaven has become more real, and my longing for its joy is more fierce than ever before.

# 6 Conclusion

*The city has no need of sun or moon, for the glory of God illuminates the city, and the Lamb is its light. The nations of the earth will walk in its light, and the rulers of the world will come and bring their glory to it. Its gates never close at the end of day because there is no night. And all the nations will bring their glory and honor into the city.*

REVELATION 21:23-26

Some say heaven is just "pie in the sky," a flimsy fantasy for religious dreamers. Others picture a sappy greeting-card kind of existence where we all become angels, strumming blissfully on harps while floating aimlessly on the clouds. Those people wonder why anyone would want to spend eternity in such a boring place. Some find it difficult to think about heaven because they are too attached to the world as they know it. The Bible teaches, largely through prophecy, that heaven is not only real but so glorious and exciting that it makes our present earthly existence seem pale, threadbare, and utterly dull by comparison. First Corinthians 2:9 says: "No eye has seen, no ear has heard, and no mind has imagined what God has prepared for those who love him." Heaven is the eternal experience of true joy for which we were created, the fullness of love for which we spend our earthly life searching, and the restoration and re-creation of all that Satan and sin have destroyed. Heaven is the everlasting adventure of living in the glory of God and serving our victorious King.

The sure hope of heaven sustains believers in the midst of hardship, comforts them in suffering, and allows them to face death with peace and confidence. The beauty and joy of heaven call the believer to share the good news of the gospel of Jesus Christ with a hopeless world. The wondrous God of heaven fills the church's worship with joy and wonder. And heaven is the reality to which so much of prophecy points.

In Acts chapter 7 we read the story of Stephen, the first Christian martyr. In the months after Christ's death and resurrection, Stephen became one of the leaders of the early Christian church. He boldly preached the good news of salvation through Christ. Soon he was falsely accused of blaspheming God and Moses and was brought before the high council. At his trial Stephen responded to his interrogation by delivering a powerful message in which he charged the Jewish leaders with the murder of their Messiah. His accusers were enraged and dragged him away to be stoned. As the stones rained down and his life ebbed away, we read that Stephen, "full of the Holy Spirit, gazed steadily upward into heaven and saw the glory of God, and he saw Jesus standing in the place of honor at God's right hand" (Acts 7:55).

This is the only place in the Bible where Jesus is said to be *standing* at the right hand of God. In every other reference to Christ in heaven, he is *seated* in the position of honor at God's right hand. Why is he standing here? Perhaps the Lord Jesus is standing to honor and welcome his beloved child Stephen to the place he has prepared for him. And maybe this text is suggesting that the Lord himself will rise to greet each one who has trusted him as Savior and Lord. The point is, one way or another, we will meet Jesus Christ face-to-face. Either we will meet him at the moment of our death, or he will meet us when he comes again. May we one day share Stephen's honor of seeing our King stand to welcome us into his heaven.

*Amen! Come, Lord Jesus!*

REVELATION 22:20

# An Invitation

I hope that reading this book has not only helped you understand more about Bible prophecy but has also caused you to think seriously about your relationship to God. If Jesus were to return today, would you be fully prepared to meet him? If you were to stand before God today, what reason would you give that you should enter into heaven for all eternity?

If you have always assumed that "being a good person" was the requirement for heaven, you now know that that would be a totally inadequate response. The Bible says we have all sinned and that our sins have separated us from a holy and loving God. No one is good enough to qualify for heaven. The only way to be fully prepared is to depend completely on the grace and mercy of God expressed through Jesus Christ. If you would like to be absolutely certain that you are prepared for Christ's return—if you want to be sure that you will, indeed, inherit eternal life when you die—you can do that in the next few moments. Here's how:

1. *First, you need to recognize and acknowledge that you are a sinner in need of forgiveness.*

For all have sinned; all fall short of God's glorious standard. Yet now God in his gracious kindness declares us not guilty. He has done this through Christ Jesus, who has freed us by taking away our sins. (Romans 3:23-24)

2. *You must repent of your sin—that is, turn away from anything in your life that you know to be wrong—and resolve to walk in a path that is obedient to Christ.*

Each of you must turn from your sins and turn to God. (Acts 2:38)

3. *You must ask Christ, through the power of the Holy Spirit, to give you spiritual rebirth and to come and live in you.* Jesus said,

I assure you, unless you are born again, you can never see the Kingdom of God. (John 3:3)

Look! Here I stand at the door and knock. If you hear me calling and open the door, I will come in. (Revelation 3:20)

4. *You must commit yourself completely to knowing, loving, and serving Christ for the rest of your life.* The apostle Paul said,

I am focusing all my energies on this one thing: Forgetting the past and looking forward to what lies ahead, I strain to reach the end of the race and receive the prize for which God, through Christ Jesus, is calling us up to heaven. (Philippians 3:13-14)

I invite and encourage you to begin your new life with Christ by doing the above things. One of the ways to do that is to talk to God and tell him that you want to do

that. You might want to pray something
like this:

*Dear God,*
*I acknowledge that I have sinned and that*
*I fall well short of your standard of perfect*
*goodness and holiness. I know now that I can-*
*not save myself by good works. I believe that*
*Jesus Christ is your Son, that he died on the*
*cross to pay the penalty for my sin, that he rose*
*from the dead to give me the hope of eternal*
*life, and that one day he will return to take me*
*to be with him in heaven forever. Lord, I ask*
*you to forgive my sins. Please send your Holy*
*Spirit into my life and begin to teach me and*
*shape me as you wish. I commit myself to*
*knowing, loving, and serving you for the rest of*
*my life. Please help me to do that. In the name*
*of Jesus. Amen.*

You do not need to pray exactly those
words. Just talk to God honestly from your
heart. He will hear you and understand.
You may or may not feel anything special
as you talk to him, but if you truly want to
belong to Christ, rest assured that he will

welcome you into his family of believers. Think of it—the God of the universe, who created you, will forgive all your sins and make you a new person! He will live in you by his Spirit and be your loving Savior and Lord. He will guide you throughout this life and welcome you into heaven. The Bible says that if you have repented of your sins and asked God to save you and make you his, the angels in heaven are rejoicing over you (Luke 15:10).

If you are a new Christian, I want to encourage you to do two things: First, begin to read your Bible, and talk to God every day. Prayer is simply talking honestly with God. As you do that, you will begin to discover that God also communicates with you by the Holy Spirit. If you don't have a Bible, I encourage you to purchase one of the new translations that includes helpful study notes. Second, I encourage you to commit yourself to finding a local church, where you can share in the weekly worship, learn from the teaching, and enjoy getting to know God's people there. It may take some time to find just the right church for you, but make it a top priority to do so. Those people can encourage you in your new life and help you to grow in your faith as a child of God.

May God bless you richly as you begin your journey of faith with him!

—Brian Coffey

# Appendix: Definition of Terms

Part of the difficulty surrounding the subject of Christ's return stems from the fact that throughout the centuries, Bible scholars and theologians have developed several different theories of eschatology. Although it is not the purpose of this book to describe each position in detail or to endorse one position over another, it can be helpful to become familiar with each view in a nutshell. In this section, you will find some general definitions of terms related to Bible prophecy.

## The Rapture

Shortly before his arrest and crucifixion, Jesus predicted his death and promised his disciples that one day he would return to take them to be with him. The New Testament indicates that when Christ returns, Christians who have already died will experience a physical resurrection of their body, and those still living at that time will rise from the earth to meet the Lord in the air. The *Rapture* refers to that taking up of the saints (all Christians) to meet Christ at the time of his return:

> We who are still living when the Lord returns will not rise to meet him ahead of those who are in their graves. For the Lord himself will come down from heaven with a commanding shout, with the call of the archangel, and with the trumpet call of God. First, all the Christians who have died will rise from their graves. Then, together with them, we who are still alive and remain on the earth will be caught up in the clouds to meet the Lord in the air and remain with him forever. So comfort and encourage each other with these words. (1 Thessalonians 4:15-18)

There is considerable mystery surrounding this event. In some parts of the New Testament, we read that when a Christian dies, he or she goes immediately into the presence of God. For example, in 2 Corinthians 5:8 Paul writes: "We would rather be away from these bodies, for then we will be at home with the Lord." If believers go immediately to be with the Lord, how is it that they will rise again when Christ returns? Most scholars resolve this dilemma by assuming that when believers die, their spirits go immediately to heaven, but at the Rapture their dead and decomposed physical bodies will be raised and transformed into the eternal spiritual bodies we read about in 1 Corinthians 15: "Our earthly bodies, which die and decay, will be different when they are resurrected, for they will never die. Our bodies now disappoint us, but when they are raised, they will be full of glory" (1 Corinthians 15:42-43).

## The Millennium

The *Millennium* refers to a thousand-year reign of Christ and his people, mentioned in Revelation 20.

> I saw an angel come down from heaven with the key to the bottomless pit and a heavy chain in his hand. He seized the

> dragon—that old serpent, the Devil,
> Satan—and bound him in chains for a
> thousand years. . . . And I saw the souls
> of those who had not worshiped the
> beast. . . . They came to life again, and
> they reigned with Christ for a thousand
> years. . . . They will be priests of God
> and of Christ and will reign with him a
> thousand years. (Revelation 20:1-6)

Some Christian scholars hold a
*premillennial* position: That is, they believe
Scripture indicates that Christ will return
before the Millennium to inaugurate the
one thousand years of rule on earth, during which time Satan is bound, before the
final judgment.

Others take a *postmillennial* position:
That is, they believe that the Millennium
will come before Christ's return and that
during that time the church's efforts at
evangelism will result in extraordinary
success for the gospel, with great numbers
of people coming to faith in Christ before
he returns.

Still others understand the millennial

rule of Christ figuratively. They believe the Millennium is the rule of Christ in the hearts of individual believers, or the reign of Christ in his church. Those who take this view are called *amillennialists;* they do not believe in a literal thousand-year rule of Christ on earth.

## The Tribulation

The most intriguing and controversial issue related to Bible prophecy concerns the timing of events related to Christ's return. That is because the Bible speaks not only of a glorious, thousand-year reign of Christ but also of a time of horrible suffering called the *Tribulation.* The Old Testament prophet Jeremiah described such a time: "In all history there has never been such a time of terror. It will be a time of trouble for my people Israel. Yet in the end, they will be saved!" (Jeremiah 30:7). And in the New Testament, Jesus prophesied, "That will be a time of greater horror than anything the world has ever seen or will ever see again" (Matthew 24:21).

Many scholars believe these prophetic

passages refer to the *Great Tribulation*—
seven years of world suffering and destruction at the hands of the Antichrist. While
it is clear that God intends to take up his
church to be with him forever, what is less
clear is the timing of the Rapture. Scripture plainly teaches that, prior to the
Lord's actual return to earth, there will be
a period of intense worldwide trouble such
as no generation has ever experienced.
The time of unimaginable upheaval and
suffering is known as the Great Tribulation. The questions Bible scholars and
theologians struggle to answer are: Will
Christians remain in the world during the
Tribulation and endure the fury of Satan's
final onslaught with the rest of the world?
Will Christ return to take his people from
the world before the Tribulation? Or does
the answer lie somewhere between the
two?

## *The Pre-Tribulation Interpretation*

This view teaches that the rapture of the
church will take place *before* the Tribulation. Typically the view of more conserva-

tive scholars, the pre-Tribulation position comes from the book of Revelation: "Because you have obeyed my command to persevere, I will protect you from the great time of testing that will come upon the whole world to test those who belong to this world" (Revelation 3:10). Pre-Tributationists interpret this text to mean that God promises to spare Christians from that time of suffering by rescuing them from the world before the Tribulation begins. Furthermore, the church is clearly the focus of the first three chapters of Revelation but is not mentioned after the detailed description of worldwide destruction and turmoil. Therefore, those holding the pre-Tribulation position typically believe that the rapture of the church will take place *prior* to the Tribulation, and that the second coming of Christ will be a distinct event that occurs *after* the Tribulation.

To hold the pre-Tribulation position is to believe that the return of Christ is imminent, that it could occur at any time. If this position is correct, the Lord could return before you finish reading this book!

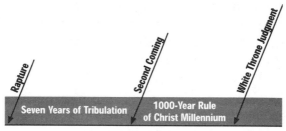

World History
**Pre-Tribulation Timeline**

### *The Post-Tribulation and Mid-Tribulation Interpretations*

These views hold that Christ will return either *after* the Tribulation (post-Tribulation) or partway through it (mid-Tribulation), and, therefore, Christians will go through all or part of the Tribulation with the rest of the world before Christ returns for his people. Post-Tribulationists believe the church will endure a literal seven-year time of worldwide catastrophe, suffering, and death, and that only after this time of suffering will Christ return to remove his church through the Rapture. Some in this category look at the history of persecution and martyrdom of Christians throughout the ages (and even now in many parts of the world) and believe that the Tribulation described in Revelation refers to all of that suffering, not just to a specific seven-year period. In this view, the return of Christ may or may not be imminent, depending on whether one believes the Tribulation has already begun. Most holding the post-Tribulation view believe that the Rapture and the second coming of Christ will occur simultaneously and will inaugurate the millennial kingdom of Christ.

Mid-Tribulationists use the prophecy in Daniel that speaks of a period lasting half of a set of seven to suggest that the church will experience only the first three and a half years of the Tribulation (Daniel 9:27). Those who hold this view believe that Christ will return after that three-and-a-half-year period to take his church out of the world.

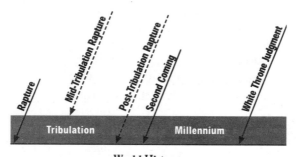

World History

**Post-Tribulation/Mid-Tribulation Timeline**

## The Great White Throne Judgment

The *Great White Throne Judgment* will be
God's final judgment on all humanity.
God's seemingly endless patience with
unbelief and sin will come to an end, and
he will reward each person according to
his or her deeds. Only those whose names
appear in the Book of Life, that is, those
whose sins have been forgiven by the
mercy of Christ, will be spared:

> I saw a great white throne, and I saw
> the one who was sitting on it. The
> earth and sky fled from his presence,
> but they found no place to hide. I saw

the dead, both great and small, standing before God's throne. And the books were opened, including the Book of Life. And the dead were judged according to the things written in the books, according to what they had done. (Revelation 20:11-12)

# Notes

## Introduction

1. Elizabeth Gleick, "The Marker We've Been Waiting For," *Time*, 7 April 1997.

## Chapter 1: Prophecy and the Past: The End of the World As We Know It

1. John F. Walvoord, *The Final Drama* (Grand Rapids: Kregel Publications, 1997), 6.
2. Ibid., 8.
3. Timothy P. Weber, Ph.D., *The Future Explored* (Colorado Springs: Victor Books, 1978), 21.

## Chapter 2: Prophecy and the Future: The King of Kings and the Great Enemy

1. Hal Lindsay, *The 1980's: Countdown to Armageddon* (Portland, Me.: Westgate Press, 1980), 8.
2. Weber, *The Future Explored,* 57.
3. Ibid., 51.

4. Rob Lindsted, Ph.D., *The Next Move* (Wichita, Kan.: Bible Truth, 1985), 4.
5. Ibid., 5.

# Chapter 3: Prophecy and Preparation: The Second Coming—Ready or Not?

1. Weber, *The Future Explored*, 30–31.
2. George Barna, *What Americans Believe* (Ventura, Calif.: Regal Books, 1991), 174.
3. Ibid., 175.

# Chapter 4: Prophecy and Eternity: Heaven—My Father's House

1. David Van Biema, "Does Heaven Exist?" *Time*, 31 March 1997.
2. C. S. Lewis, *Mere Christianity* (New York: Macmillan, 1952), 20.
3. C. S. Lewis, *The Great Divorce* (New York: Macmillan, 1945).
4. Vera C. Rubin, "Galaxy," *Microsoft Encarta '96 Encyclopedia* (Funk & Wagnalls, 1993–1995).
5. David Wells, quoted in David Van Biema, "Does Heaven Exist?" *Time*, 24 March 1997.

6. Peter Kreeft, *Everything You Ever Wanted to Know about Heaven—But Never Dreamed of Asking* (San Francisco: Ignatius Press, 1990), 19.
7. C. S. Lewis, *The Problem of Pain* (New York: Macmillan, 1944), 141–42.
8. Erwin Lutzer, *One Minute after You Die* (Chicago: Moody Press, 1997), 89.

## Chapter 5: Going Home!

1. Alice Gray, comp., *Stories for the Heart* (Sisters, Oreg.: Questar Press/Multnomah Books, 1996), 112.
2. Kreeft, *Everything You Ever Wanted to Know about Heaven,* 197.

# Suggested Reading

Tim LaHaye and Jerry B. Jenkins, *Left Behind, Tribulation Force, Nicolae, Soul Harvest, Apollyon,* and *Assassins* (Wheaton, Ill.: Tyndale House Publishers).

Peter and Paul LaLonde, *2000 A.D.: Are You Ready?* (Nashville: Thomas Nelson Publishers, 1997).

C. S. Lewis, *Mere Christianity* (New York: Simon & Schuster, 1997).

C. S. Lewis, *The Great Divorce* (New York: Simon & Schuster, 1996).

Robert P. Lightner, *The Last Days Handbook* (Nashville: Thomas Nelson Publishers, 1997).

Josh McDowell, *More Than a Carpenter* (Wheaton, Ill.: Tyndale House Publishers, 1980).

John Van Diest, *Ten Reasons Why Jesus Is Coming Soon* (Sisters, Oreg.: Multnomah Books, 1998).

John F. Walvoord, *The Final Drama* (Grand Rapids: Kregel Publications, 1993).

# About the Author

Brian Coffey is senior pastor of First
Baptist Church of Geneva (Illinois). He
is the author of *Splendor in the Ordinary*
(Tyndale, 1993) and has written study
notes for the *TouchPoint Bible* (Tyndale,
1996) and *The Rock* (Tyndale, 1998). He
and his wife, Lorene, live in Batavia,
Illinois, with their four sons, Jordan, Jesse,
Micah, and Canaan.